Chess Tactics for Kids

Murray Chandler

THE SKEWER

First published in the UK by Gambit Publications Ltd 2003
Reprinted 2004, 2006, 2007, 2008, 2010, 2012, 2014, 2016, 2017, 2021, 2022

ISBN-13: 978-1-901983-99-9
ISBN-10: 1-901983-99-4

DISTRIBUTION:
Worldwide (except USA): Central Books Ltd, 50 Freshwater Rd, Chadwell Heath, London RM8 1RX.
Tel +44 (0)20 8986 4854 Fax +44 (0)20 8533 5821. E-mail: orders@Centralbooks.com
Gambit Publications Ltd, 27 Queens Pine, Bracknell, Berks, RG12 0TL, England.

E-mail: info@gambitbooks.com
Website (regularly updated): www.gambitbooks.com

Edited by Graham Burgess
Typeset by Petra Nunn
Printed in the USA by Sheridan MN

20 19 18 17 16 15 14 13 12

Dedication: better be to my Mum! Plus, of course, her grandchildren: Alex, Sam, Ben, and Lara, Matthew and Olivia.
Acknowledgements: David Stanley (cover), Helen Milligan (proofreading and suggestions).
Illustrations: Cindy McCluskey

Gambit Publications Ltd
Directors: Dr John Nunn GM, Murray Chandler GM and Graham Burgess FM
German Editor: Petra Nunn WFM
Bookkeeper: Andrea Burgess

Contents

The 50 Tricky Tactics

DEFLECTION

Introduction

The best way to confound and confuse a chess opponent is by using *tactics* – a forcing sequence of moves that gain an advantage. This book aims to help you do this, by showing combinations that arise from typical piece formations. Recognizing these patterns will improve your tactical ability, enabling you to win your opponent's pawns and pieces with ease when such possibilities arise.

This collection of 50 Tricky Tactics deals with tactical manoeuvres (such as forks and pins), and also with thematic combinations that win material. It is written as a complementary sequel to my previous book, *How to Beat Your Dad at Chess*, which covered checkmating patterns. From the amazing reception the DAD book received, it seems the coverage of pattern recognition has really touched a chord amongst ordinary players. There is no reason why juniors, home or club players can't learn these patterns, and so make the same – sometimes astonishing – mental shortcuts that the top masters do.

Only themes which arise fairly frequently in actual practice have been included[1]. Before too long I'm sure that you will be springing many of these tactical traps on your friends and club mates, or perhaps even on your long-suffering Dad.

Murray Chandler

---

1 OK, I confess to one exception, Tricky Tactic 29 (Kamikaze Queen and Rampant Rook). This motif is rare, but is so fantastic I just couldn't resist putting it in.

Algebraic Notation

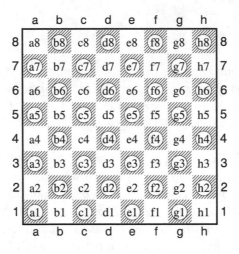

The chess notation used in this book is the simple, algebraic notation in use throughout the world. It can be learnt by anyone in just a few minutes.

As you can see from the chessboard above, the files are labelled a-h (going from left to right) and the ranks are labelled 1-8. This gives each square its own unique reference point. The pieces are described as follows:

Knight   =   ♞

Bishop   =   ♝

Rook   =   ♜

Queen   =   ♛

King   =   ♚

Pawns are not given a symbol. When they move simply the *destination square* is given.

The following additional symbols are also used:

Check   =   +
Double Check   =   ++
Capture   =   x
Castles kingside   =   0-0
Castles queenside =   0-0-0
Good move   =   !
Bad move   =   ?

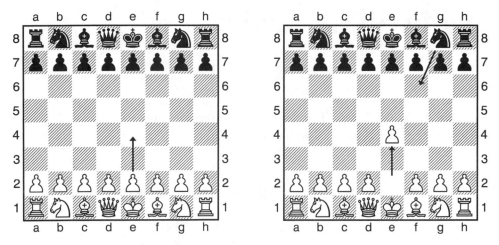

In the left-hand diagram above White is about to play the move **1 e4**. The **1** indicates the move number, and **e4** the destination square of the white pawn.

In the right-hand diagram White's **1 e4** move is complete. Black is about to reply **1...♘f6** (moving his knight to the **f6-square** on his *first move*).

THE PIN

7

How to Study Tactics

There are three key stages to becoming a master chess tactician:
1) Learn the Basic Tactical Devices (such as forks and pins).
2) Recognize typical patterns where combinations are likely to occur.
3) Combine motifs to outcalculate the opponent.

Stage One: Learn the Basic Tactical Devices

In this book we cover the most basic tactical motifs in chess:

Forks	**Discovered Checks**
Pins	**Double Checks**
Skewers	**Desperado Sacrifices**
Decoys	**Stalemates**
Deflections	**Zwischenzugs**
Overloads	**Perpetual Checks**
Discovered Attacks	**Breaking the Pin**

Being familiar with these motifs is helpful when it comes to finding combinations. In fact these themes are quite easy to learn, and even beginners will already have encountered some of the ideas. Each of these themes is explained and covered as a Tricky Tactic in this book.

Stage Two: Recognize Typical Patterns

Perhaps the biggest secret to becoming an expert at chess tactics is to *recognize positions where combinations are likely to occur*. Strong players know that certain piece formations make some tactical combinations much more common.

REMOVING A
DEFENDER

Here is a typical example, giving the bare minimum of pieces to illustrate the theme:

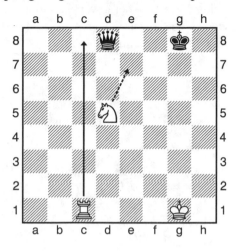

1) White moves

Experienced players will instantly spot that White wins the black queen with 1 ♖c8 ♕xc8 2 ♘e7+. This rook decoy sacrifice, followed by a knight fork, is easy to see, as the key pieces form a known pattern. You can see similar combinations in Tricky Tactic 13.

There are many such recurring tactical traps amongst the 50 Tricky Tactics in this book. One of the simplest, yet most elegant, is the Rook Endgame Skewer (Tricky Tactic 35):

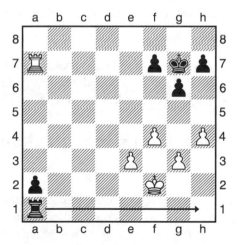

2) Black moves

The win goes 1...♖h1 (threatening to promote the pawn) 2 ♖xa2 ♖h2+ winning the white rook. Even if you do not get to play such a combination on the board, knowing the theme could be important when deciding whether or not to enter certain rook endings.

Chess Tactics for Kids is intended to show themes, not specific traps. However, a number of the Tricky Tactics do feature some very devious traps that occur via specific openings, due to the pawn or piece formations that arise. However, all of these traps can be sprung *from a variety of different positions*.

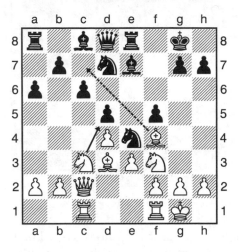

3) White moves

1 ♘xd5 wins, due to 1...cxd5 2 ♗c7 trapping the black queen.

This idea (from Tricky Tactic 49) typically arises from a Queen's Gambit Declined. Over the years, players of the black pieces have found wonderfully inventive ways to fall victim to this ♘xd5 motif! Therefore I regard this combination as a motif, rather than an opening trap.

Any of the previous three combinations could snare an inexperienced or unwary opponent. However, you might wonder how two alert, strong players, playing each other, could use a tactic to win. This question takes us on to our third stage.

Stage 3: Combining Motifs to Outcalculate the Opponent

Outcalculating a good chess-player requires a deep combination. The key is to combine several different tactical motifs in the one combination. Actually, most combinations – even simple ones – already feature more than one theme. Some brilliant and well-disguised combinations can contain a fantastic mixture of themes, making the trap easy to miss – until it is too late.

Here is a combination played in a United States Amateur Team competition. The question is: was the pawn capture with 1 ♘xe5 a good move?

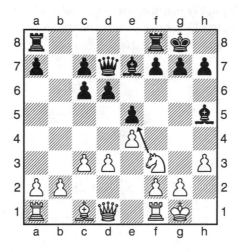

4a) White moves

The game continuation was **1 ♘xe5 dxe5 2 ♕xh5 ♕xd3 3 ♕xe5 ♗d6 4 ♕d4 ♕b5** and White had won a pawn.

At first glance it might appear that Black had simply played poorly earlier on, to allow the *breaking of the pin* with 1 ♘xe5 by White. However, a closer look reveals that there are several tactical motifs hidden below the surface – including *deflection and discovered attack* – that were never played out on the board. It is possible that Black had seen quite deeply, and was outfoxed by White, who had seen further still!

Let's analyse the combination in slow motion, starting after **1 ♘xe5** *(4b)*.

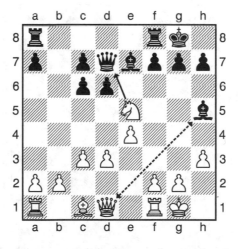

4b) Black moves

It is soon clear that White's unpinning move (1 ♘xe5) works if Black captures the white queen. White in turn would capture the black queen with advantage (1...♗xd1 2 ♘xd7).

11

Next to consider and quickly dismiss is a *desperado* defence for Black (after 1...♕xh3 2 gxh3 ♗xd1 3 ♘xc6 both black bishops are under attack). So play continues as in the game: **1...dxe5 2 ♕xh5 ♕xd3 3 ♕xe5 ♗d6 4 ♕d4** *(4c)*.

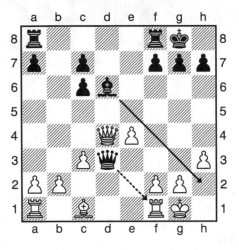

4c) Black moves

A critical moment. In the game Black conceded he had lost a pawn (retreating with 4...♕b5), after which it is clear that White's combination has succeeded. But perhaps Black's original intention here was different – to play the deflecting sacrifice **4...♗h2+**, which would win a white rook after **5 ♔xh2 ♕xf1** *(4d)*.

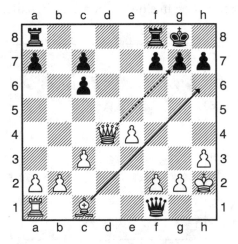

4d) White moves

This is a clever idea by Black, but as we are about to see, the story is not yet over. White has the killer response **6 ♗h6!** *(4e)*, which creates a winning *discovered attack* on the black queen!

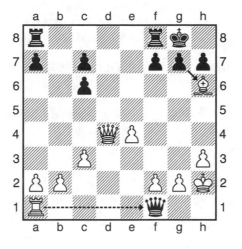

4e) Black moves

The white threat of 7 ♕xg7 mate must be attended to. After **6...gxh6** White plays **7 ♖xf1** winning the black queen.[1]

The above combination was a wonderful example of how to win by seeing further than the opponent. Practising tactical motifs and recognizing typical patterns will help you to analyse quicker, deeper and more accurately.

Finally, I should add that every Tricky Tactic position in this book is from a real game (including the tests at the end). Often Black is to move (in some chess books the position is always given with White to move). I believe it is important that these diagrams are from real life, not artificially composed. This assists in developing both pattern recognition, and also a sense of intuition as to when combinations are likely to succeed.

OVERLOADED

---

1 There were four different motifs used in this combination (Deflection, Discovered Attack, Desperado Sacrifice & Breaking the Pin). They can be seen in Tricky Tactics 8, 10, 24, and 48.

<table>
<tr><td>

**TRICKY
TACTIC** **1**

</td><td>

Forks

</td></tr>
</table>

Spearing pieces on two or more prongs...

A fork occurs where a single piece creates a successful double attack against two (or more) enemy pieces. The defender faces at least two threats, and cannot deal with them both in the space of one move.

Any piece can administer a fork. Queens and knights are sensationally good at them; surprising an opponent with a pawn fork is harder. The long-range bishop is reasonably effective. Rook forks are rare until ranks and files start opening up in the late middlegame.

Typical Position for a Pawn Fork

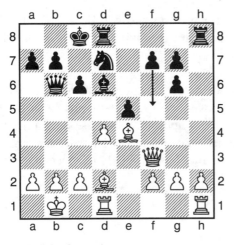

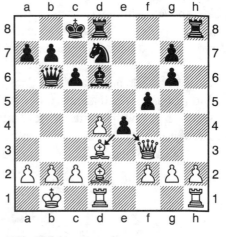

1a) Black moves

After 1...f5, White must retreat with 2 ♗d3 to save the bishop. Black continues with the pawn advance 2...e4 *(1b)*.

1b) White moves

The white queen and bishop are forked by the black pawn on e4. White loses material to the double attack.

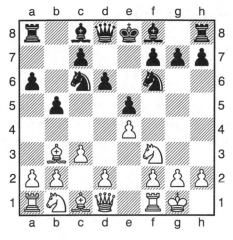

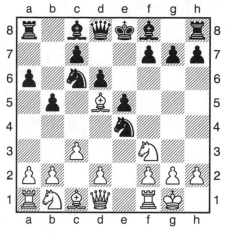

2a) Black moves

The pawn grab 1...♘xe4? is a blunder. Disaster strikes when White responds 2 ♗d5 (2b), a bishop fork.

2b) Black moves

Both unprotected black knights are simultaneously attacked by the white bishop. One of the knights will be lost.

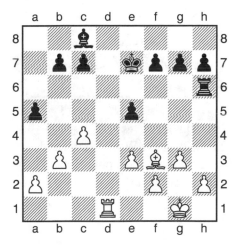

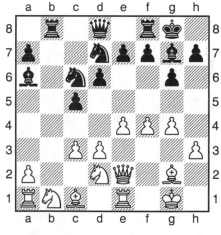

3) White moves

Rook forks occur mostly in or near the endgame. Here 1 ♖d5 wins a pawn, with a double attack on e5 and a5.

4) Black moves

The strong advance 1...♘d4! is facilitated by a bishop fork: 2 cxd4 ♗xd4+ is a double attack on the white king on g1 and rook on a1.

Knight Forks

The octopus of the chessboard

Knights are magnificent at forking, because they move in a unique way. This means that they are able to fork even the most powerful pieces without coming under return attack. A knight is able to attack many pieces at the same time (including two rooks, a queen and a king). There is even a term – 'Family Fork' – to describe this kind of multiple attack.

Typical Position for a Knight Fork

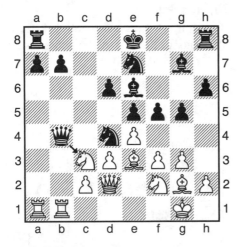

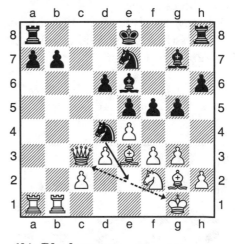

1a) Black moves

The temporary queen sacrifice 1...♛xc3 captures a knight and lures the white queen onto a forking square after 2 ♕xc3 *(1b)*.

1b) Black moves

2...♞e2+ forks White's king and queen. After the king moves out of check, Black emerges a piece ahead, i.e. 3 ♔f1 ♞xc3.

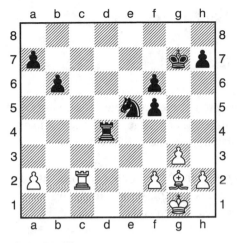

2a) Black moves

This knight fork is camouflaged. Only after 1...♖d1+ 2 ♗f1 ♘f3+! *(2b)* does the target appear.

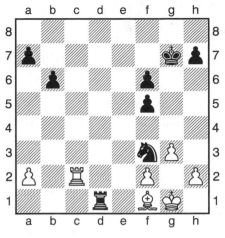

2b) White moves

White's rook on c2 will be lost to a knight fork, after either 3 ♔g2 ♘e1+ or 3 ♔h1 ♖xf1+ 4 ♔g2 ♘c1+.

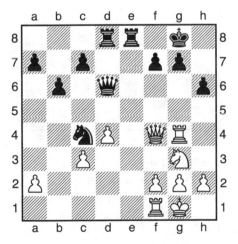

3) White moves

1 ♖xg7+ wins. If 1...♔xg7 White has the killer knight fork 2 ♘f5+, winning the black queen.

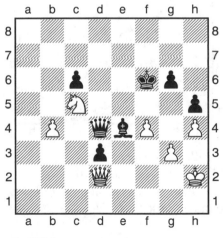

4) White moves

The clever temporary queen sacrifice 1 ♕c3! decides. On 1...♕xc3 comes the fork 2 ♘xe4+ followed by 3 ♘xc3.

Queen Forks

Long range a speciality

Although there are elementary opening traps where a queen fork can win material, the queen is really in its element in the late middlegame and endgame. Once the game opens up, this powerful piece is perfect for picking off unprotected pieces and pawns at long range.

This is especially the case if the enemy king is vulnerable to checks. In examples 3 and 4 below, it is instructive how Black first sacrifices to expose the white king. A queen fork follows soon after, regaining the investment with interest.

Typical Positions for a Queen Fork

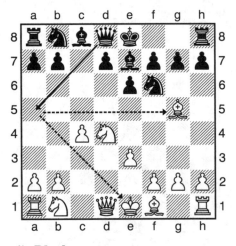

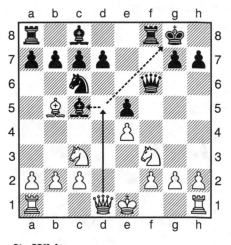

1) Black moves

A few moves into the opening, White has blundered. The bishop on g5 is lost to the queen fork 1...♕a5+.

2) White moves

1 ♕d5+ creates a double attack by checking the black king, and attacking the bishop on c5. Black is forked and loses the bishop.

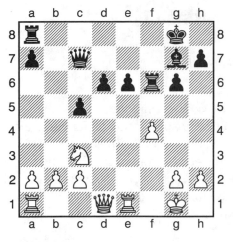

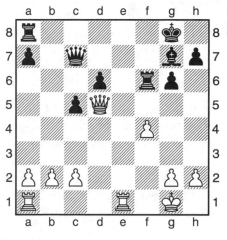

3a) White moves

The knight advance 1 ♘d5! attacks both queen and rook, so Black accepts the sacrifice: 1...exd5 2 ♕xd5+ *(3b)*.

3b) Black moves

The white queen forks the black king and rook. Whichever way Black escapes from check, White captures with 3 ♕xa8+ next move.

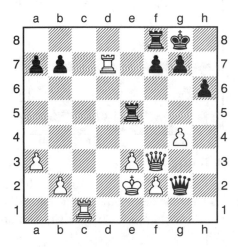

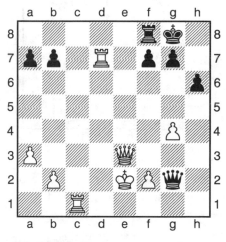

4a) Black moves

Masterful play from the game Dao-Kasparov, Batumi 2001. First 1...♖xe3+! forces 2 ♕xe3 *(4b)* (since 2 ♔xe3 loses to 2...♖e8+ 3 ♔f4 g5+).

4b) Black moves

Now White's king is exposed. 2...♕xg4+ forks the white king on e2 and the white rook on d7. Black wins two pawns.

Pins (1)

Pins for the rank and file...

A pin makes it undesirable – or impossible – for a defending piece to move, as this would expose another more valuable piece to attack. A pin occurs along either a file, rank or diagonal, so only bishops, rooks and queens can pin other pieces.

An *absolute pin* involves the enemy king. The piece in front is attacked and pinned against the king. It cannot escape, because the king would then be exposed to check. Where the king is not involved, it is technically possible for a defender to 'break the pin'. Whether this is good or not depends on the position.

Typical Positions for a Pin along a File

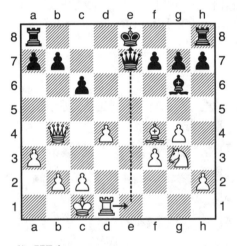

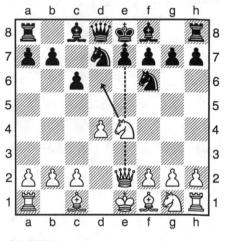

1) White moves

The rook move 1 ♖e1 pins the black queen against the black king. The black queen cannot move out of attack and is lost.

2) White moves

Another absolute pin: 1 ♘d6 is checkmate. The black e-pawn cannot capture the knight due to a pin (by White's queen on e2).

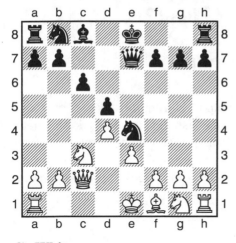

3) White moves

1 ♘xd5 exploits a pin along the c-file. Black can 'break the pin' with 1...cxd5, but 2 ♕xc8+ remains advantageous to White.

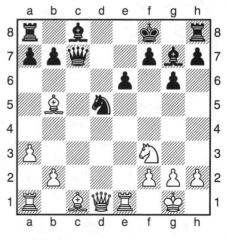

4) White moves

A mate threat means Black's e6-pawn is pinned, so 1 ♕xd5! wins a piece. If Black recaptures with 1...cxd5, then 2 ♖e8 is mate.

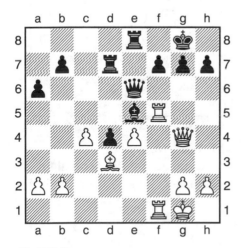

5) White moves

1 ♖xe5! wins by means of two deadly pins on the black queen. If 1...♕xg4, then 2 ♖xe8 mate, or 1...♕xe5 2 ♕xd7.

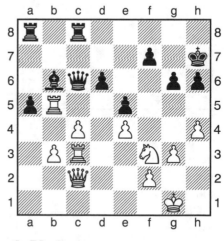

6) Black moves

1...♗d4! wins rook for bishop, due to a c-file pin. The rook cannot escape: if 2 ♖d3, then 2...♕xb5, or 2 ♘xd4 exd4 3 ♖d3 ♕xb5.

<table>
<tr><td>**TRICKY TACTIC 5**</td><td></td></tr>
</table>

TRICKY TACTIC **5**

Pins (2)

Pinning and winning

Bishops are superb at pinning – they just can't help it! During most games bishops are involved in routine pins: for example, where a white bishop pins a black knight against the black queen. Generally this represents just a minor inconvenience for the defender, and no material is lost provided the knight doesn't move.

But there are also deadlier bishop pins. As rooks and queens are so valuable, any bishop pin on a major piece is a serious matter.

Typical Position for a Pin on the Diagonal

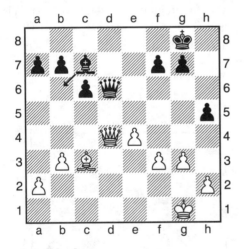

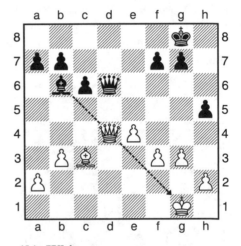

1a) Black moves

The white queen and king are exposed to a pin on the a7-g1 diagonal. Black plays 1...♗b6 *(1b)*.

1b) White moves

The white queen is lost, caught in a pin against its own king by the black bishop.

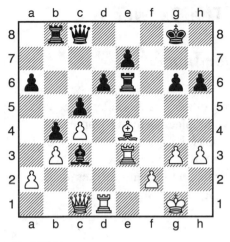

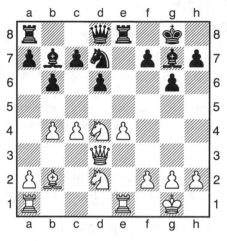

2) White moves

1 ♗d5 is a winning pin. The black rook (on e6) cannot move, as that would expose the black king on g8 to check.

3) Black moves

1...c5 exploits a pin on the long diagonal to win a piece after 2 bxc5 dxc5. If the attacked knight moves, Black has 3...♗xb2.

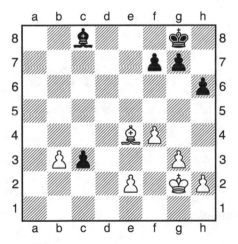

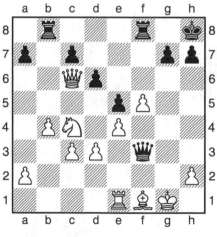

4) Black moves

The bishop sacrifice 1...♗b7! is also a pin. Black's c-pawn promotes by force after 2 ♗xb7 c2.

5) Black moves

The swindle 1...♖xf5! shows a queen doing the pinning (2 exf5 is answered by 2...♕xc6). Black's threats of 2...♕f2+ and 2...♖g5+ decide.

The Skewer

Roasted pieces for supper

A skewer attacks two enemy pieces lined up along either a rank, file or diagonal. When the valuable piece in front moves out of the way, the piece behind is captured.

Bishops are superb at skewering queens and rooks, because it does not matter if the end target is protected. A trade of bishop for rook will be advantageous anyway.

For a queen to carry out an effective skewer, the target piece must generally be unprotected. See also Tricky Tactic 35 for a really devious Rook Skewer.

Typical Positions for a Skewer

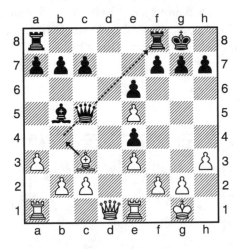

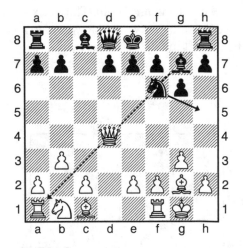

1) White moves

1 ♗b4 employs the bishop to skewer Black's queen and rook. After the attacked queen moves, the rook is captured (e.g., 1...♕xe5 2 ♗xf8).

2) Black moves

1...♘h5 unveils a skewer on the long diagonal. The valuable queen must move, and Black captures the rook on a1 with the bishop.

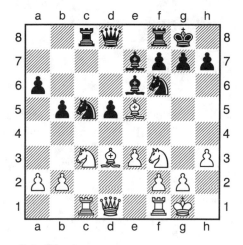

3a) Black moves

This is taken from the Petrosian-Spassky World Championship match in Moscow 1969. Black begins with 1...d4! 2 ♗xd4 ♘xd3 3 ♕xd3 *(3b)*.

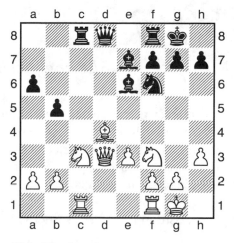

3b) Black moves

Now for the point of Black's pawn sacrifice. 3...♗c4 skewers queen and rook, winning material after 4 ♕b1 ♗xf1.

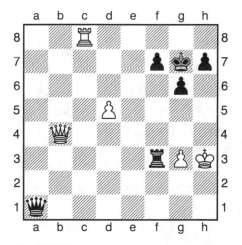

4) White moves

After 1 ♕f8+ ♔f6 the white queen administers a winning skewer of Black's king and queen: 2 ♕h8+ ♔g5 3 ♕xa1.

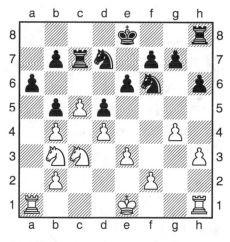

5) White moves

Back-rank skewers are common, as exploited here by 1 ♘xb5. If 1...axb5 comes a king and rook skewer: 2 ♖a8+ ♔e7 3 ♖xh8.

Decoy Sacrifices

Luring pieces to their doom

In a decoy sacrifice an enemy piece is lured – or rather forced – onto a specific square. The sacrifice can be made for several reasons, but most commonly the plan is to enable a powerful fork or pin to be carried out.

Decoys can be crushingly strong, and sometimes win the game instantly. They are often used in checkmating attacks.

Typical Position for a Decoy Sacrifice

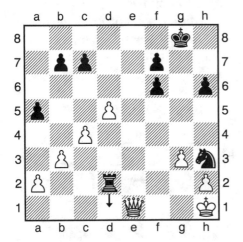

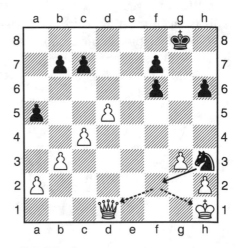

1a) Black moves

The classic rook decoy sacrifice 1...♖d1 pins the white queen, and thus forces the capture 2 ♕xd1 (*1b*).

1b) Black moves

Mission accomplished: the white queen has been decoyed to the d1-square. Black plays 2...♘f2+, a winning knight fork.

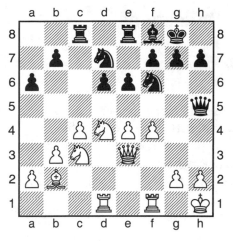

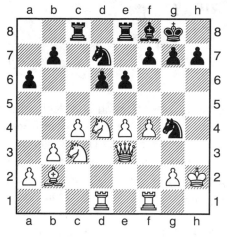

2a) Black moves

Queens and knights work well together. 1...♛xh2+! decoys the white king to a nasty forking square after 2 ♔xh2 ♞g4+ (2b).

2b) Black moves

After 3 ♔g1 (or 3 ♔h1) comes 3...♞xe3. Black has won a pawn, and as a bonus also forks the white rooks!

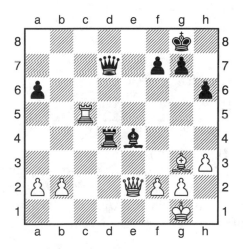

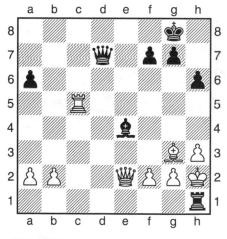

3a) Black moves

A vicious mating version: 1...♜d1+ 2 ♔h2 ♜h1+! (3b) sacrifices a rook to force White's king to the h1-square.

3b) White moves

3 ♔xh1 ♛xh3+! shows the point of the deadly decoy. The white g-pawn is pinned, and next move Black checkmates with 4...♛xg2.

<table>
<tr><td>**TRICKY**
TACTIC **8**</td><td></td><td># Deflections</td></tr>
</table>

Deflections

Send the defender packing

The terms of deflection and decoy are widely used to mean the same thing by many players. In fact there is a subtle difference between the two types of sacrifices.

In a decoy sacrifice (Tricky Tactic 7), an enemy piece is lured *onto* a very particular square. In a deflection, the enemy piece is forced *away* from a particular square. So in a deflection, it doesn't really matter where the piece is deflected to, so long as it no longer fulfils its previous defensive task.

Typical Positions for a Deflection

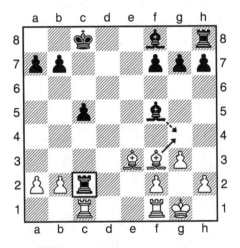

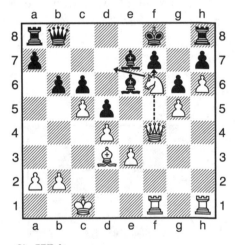

1) White moves

1 ♗g4! wins material after 1...♗xg4 2 ♖xc2. The black bishop was deflected *away* from the defence of the rook on c2.

2) White moves

1 ♘d7+ is a winning fork of king and queen. If 1...♗xd7, 2 ♕xf7 mate – the bishop is deflected *away* from its vital role of guarding f7.

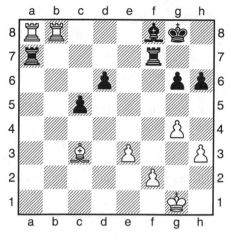

3) White moves

Instead of a rook swap on a7, 1 ♖xf8+! deflects Black's other rook from defending the a7-rook. After 1...♖xf8 2 ♖xa7 White has won a piece.

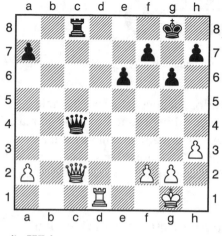

4) White moves

This old favourite continues to claim victims: 1 ♖d8+! ♔g7 (if 1...♖xd8, then 2 ♕xc4) 2 ♖xc8 wins a rook.

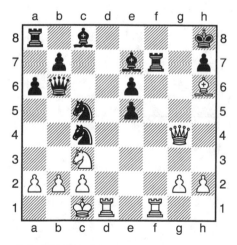

5a) White moves

Both sides have strong attacks (1 ♖xf7? allows 1...♕xb2 mate). White's rook deflection is spectacular: 1 ♖d8+! (5b) (since if 1...♕xd8, 2 ♖xf7).

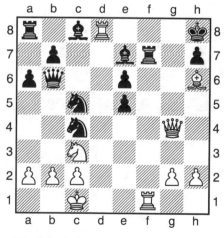

5b) Black moves

On 1...♗xd8, 2 ♗g7+! reveals the reason for deflecting the bishop – 2...♖xg7 3 ♖f8+. White also mates after 2...♔g8 3 ♗xe5+ ♔f8 4 ♕g7+.

<table>
<tr><td>

TRICKY TACTIC 9

</td><td>

Overload

</td></tr>
</table>

Piling on the pressure

Overloading occurs where a single defending piece has too many defensive tasks to fulfil. Something has to give, and so material is lost.

An Overloading combination can be very similar to a Decoy Sacrifice (Tricky Tactic 7) or a Deflection (Tricky Tactic 8), and to an extent the terms are interchangeable. The difference is that, in its purest form, no material sacrifice is involved in creating an Overload.

Typical Position for an Overload

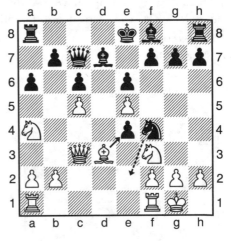

1a) Black moves

The swap 1...dxe4! *(1b)* turns out to be a winning pawn fork. The white bishop is overloaded and cannot recapture.

1b) White moves

The problem is that 2 ♗xe4 ♘e2+ forks the white king and queen. White's bishop cannot both guard e2, and capture on e4.

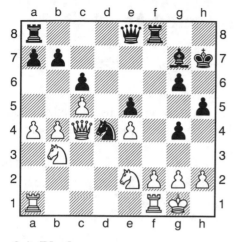

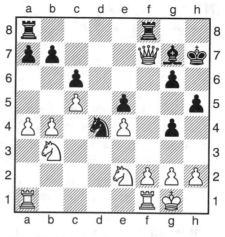

2a) Black moves

1...♕f7! overloads the white queen, and also features the themes of Deflection and Zwischenzug after 2 ♕xf7 *(2b)*.

2b) Black moves

With the white queen gone, Black inserts 2...♘xe2+ 3 ♔h1 and then recaptures with 3...♖xf7. The combination has won a piece.

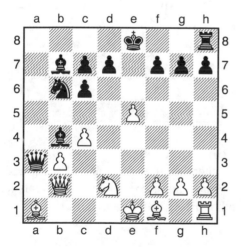

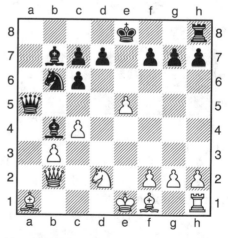

3a) Black moves

1...♕a5! *(3b)* is a surprise overload. Black wins a piece in slow motion, as the white pieces are unluckily positioned.

3b) White moves

There is no way to parry the threat of 2...♗xd2+ 3 ♕xd2 ♕xa1+. White's queen cannot maintain protection of both d2 and a1.

Discovered Attack

Revealing and dangerous

A discovered attack is a strong motif, even if not as devastating as a discovered check (as covered in the next Tricky Tactic). The principle is the same: a piece moves to unveil a hidden attack from another of your pieces.

Discovered attacks can be harnessed to win material by means of a double attack. Unlike a fork (where a single piece carries out the double attack), here two pieces create the simultaneous threats that the opponent is unable to cope with.

Typical Position for a Discovered Attack

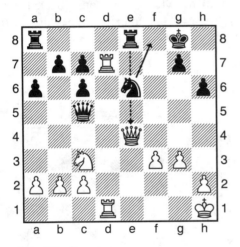

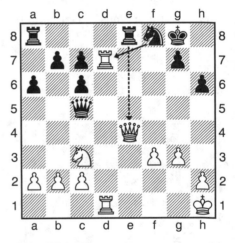

1a) Black moves

1...♘f8 *(1b)* attacks a white rook. It also uncovers a discovered attack on the white queen (from Black's rook on e8).

1b) White moves

Either the queen or rook will be captured – White cannot cope with both threats together. Black will win material.

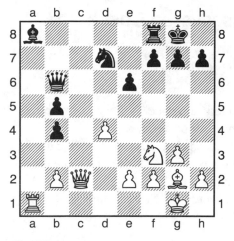

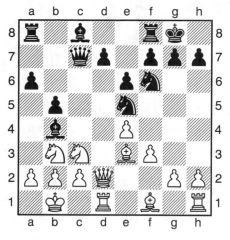

2) White moves

1 ♘g5 (threatening ♕xh7 mate) also creates a discovered attack on the black bishop. Black loses a piece; e.g., 1...♘f6 2 ♗xa8.

3) White moves

1 ♘xb5, a discovered attack on Black's bishop, nets a pawn after 1...axb5 2 ♕xb4. If 1...♗xd2, then 2 ♘xc7 ♗xe3 3 ♘xa8 wins for White.

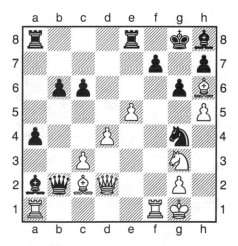

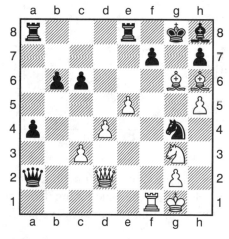

4a) White moves

1 ♖xa2! (removing a defender of the f7-square) 1...♕xa2 2 ♗xg6! *(4b)* creates a decisive discovered attack on the black queen.

4b) Black moves

White wins due to multiple threats. For example, if 2...hxg6, 3 ♕xa2, or 2...♕xd2 3 ♗xf7 mate.

Discovered Check

Like having a move for free

A discovered check is an immensely powerful tactical device. A piece moves out of the way to reveal an attack on the enemy king from another piece.

Strong players are terrified of allowing a discovered check. It is almost like giving the opponent a free move. Because the defender's king is being checked, the piece unveiling the check can move to the most astonishing squares.

Having this wide choice is what makes a discovered check so strong. At least one of the options is likely to be winning.

Typical Position for a Discovered Check

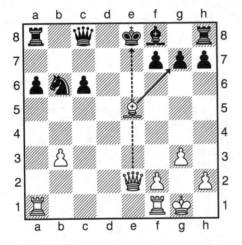

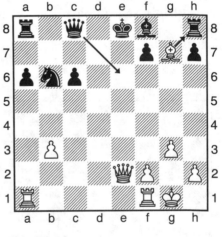

1a) White moves

Any bishop move will unveil a discovered check on the black king from the white queen. White chooses 1 ♗xg7+ *(1b)*.

1b) Black moves

As Black must attend to the check on the king, the rook on h8 will be lost. For example, 1...♕e6 2 ♕xe6+ fxe6 3 ♗xh8.

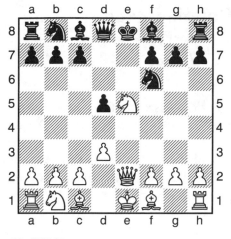

2) White moves

A beginner's trap: 1 ♘c6+ wins a queen. White's knight on c6 is immune from capture, as Black is in check along the e-file.

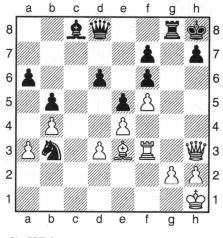

3) White moves

1 ♕xh7+ shows a thematic mating pattern: 1...♔xh7 2 ♖h3+ ♔g7 3 ♗h6+ ♔h7 (or 3...♔h8) 4 ♗f8 – discovered check and mate!

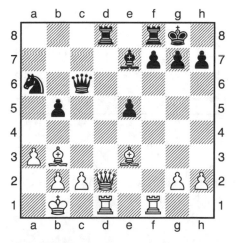

4a) White moves

A queen sacrifice brilliancy from Grandmaster Andrei Sokolov: 1 ♕xd8! ♖xd8 (if 1...♗xd8, 2 ♖xf7 wins) 2 ♖xd8+ ♗xd8 3 ♖xf7 (4b).

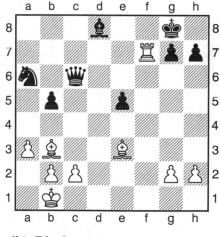

4b) Black moves

The mighty threat of a discovered check wins for White! After 3...♕e8 4 ♖e7+ ♔f8 5 ♖xe8+ ♔xe8 White is a pawn ahead.

TRICKY TACTIC 12 — Double Check

Double Check

The mother of all checks

A double check is... well, pretty frightening actually! This is a motif so powerful it often results in immediate checkmate. It occurs when two attacking pieces give check simultaneously.

When two pieces give check it is impossible for either check to be blocked, or for both checking pieces to be captured. The only option available is flight. The checked king must move.

Typical Position for a Double Check

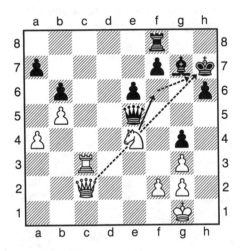

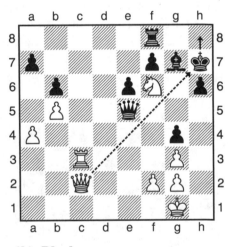

1a) White moves

1 ♘f6++ *(1b)* (1 ♘g5++ is the same) puts Black in double check. White's queen and knight are both checking the king.

1b) Black moves

The only option is for Black to move the king, but after 1...♔h8 Black is checkmated by 2 ♕h7.

36

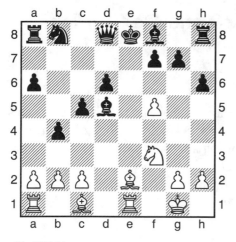

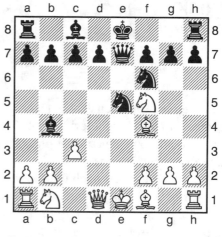

2) White moves

Although a queen down, White wins with 1 ♗b5 checkmate. Due to the double check Black is unable to interpose a defender.

3) Black moves

The black queen is under attack. This would rule out a normal discovered check, but not a double check: 1...♘f3 delivers checkmate.

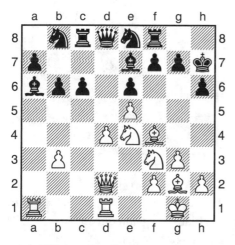

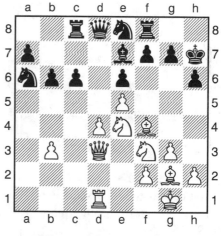

4a) White moves

A nice queen fork is facilitated by a threat of double check: 1 ♖xa6! ♘xa6 2 ♕d3 *(4b)* attacks the black knight on a6.

4b) Black moves

The knight is lost, as Black must deal with a more serious threat to his king. If 2...♘b4?, 3 ♘f6++ (or 3 ♘eg5++) 3...♚h8 4 ♕h7 mate.

The ♖c8 and ♘e7+ Trick

The lady-killer

This combination often wins a queen. It features a rook decoy sacrifice on the c8-square, followed up by a knight fork on the e7-square. The fork of the black king and queen exploits a common formation of pieces, as, following kingside castling, the black king is naturally located on the g8-square.

The ingredients to watch out for are the following:

1) *a white knight on d5 and a white rook on the open c-file;*
2) *the black queen on d8 and the black king on g8;*
3) *Black's e7-square is undefended (except by the black queen).*

Typical Pattern for the ♖xc8 and ♘xe7+ Decoy

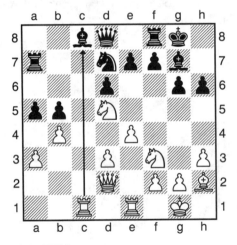 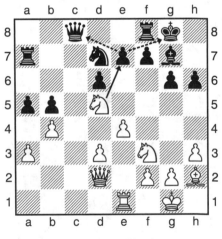

1a) White moves

First comes the rook sacrifice to decoy the black queen to the c8-square: 1 ♖xc8 ♛xc8 *(1b)*.

1b) White moves

The follow-up 2 ♘xe7+ is a knight fork of the black king and queen. After 2...♚h8 3 ♘xc8 White wins.

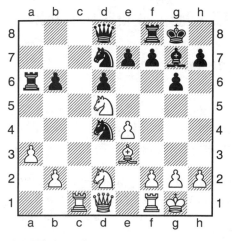

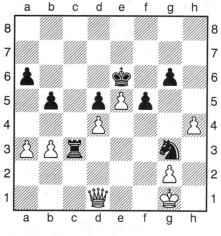

2) White moves

It is not essential to capture anything on c8. 1 ♖c8 ♕xc8 2 ♘xe7+ wins the black queen for rook and knight.

3) Black moves

The knight can start on a different square (in this case g3 rather than d4), but the principle is the same: 1...♖c1! 2 ♕xc1 ♘e2+ winning.

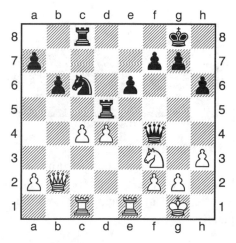

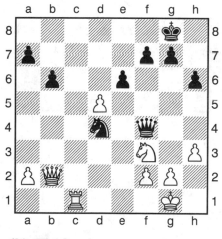

4a) Black moves

A classy example. Ignoring the fact that his rook is attacked by a pawn, Black plays 1...♘xd4! 2 cxd5 ♖xc1 3 ♖xc1 (4b).

4b) Black moves

The sacrificed material is neatly regained with 3...♕xc1+ 4 ♕xc1 ♘e2+ 5 ♔f1 ♘xc1. Black emerges a pawn up in the endgame.

The ♗xf7+ and ♘g5+ Trick

A beginner's trap that wins a pawn

If allowed, this simple tactic is normally very strong. Using a bishop sacrifice, White lures the black king to the f7-square – whereupon a knight fork regains material. If the knight fork wins back a bishop, the combination would typically win a pawn.

If the white knight threatens to fork the king and a *major* piece – a queen or rook – White's bishop sacrifice must be declined. In this case the black position is equally desperate, as the f7-pawn is lost for nothing, and the king gets misplaced too.

Typical Position for ♗xf7+ followed by ♘g5+

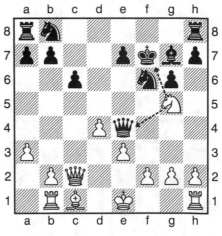

1a) White moves

1 ♗xf7+ wins a pawn. Black must decline the bishop (by playing 1...♔f8 or 1...♔d8), as on 1...♔xf7 there follows 2 ♘g5+ *(1b)*.

1b) Black moves

The white knight has administered a deadly fork. The black king must move out of check, allowing 3 ♘xe4, winning a queen.

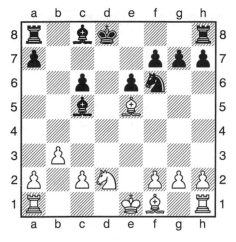

2a) Black moves

After 1...♗xf2+ the bishop sacrifice could be declined (with 2 ♔e2), but White would have lost a pawn for nothing. Therefore 2 ♔xf2 ♘g4+ *(2b)*.

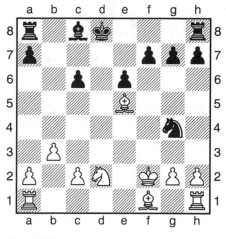

2b) White moves

A familiar knight fork appears. After the white king moves, Black ends up a pawn ahead with 3...♘xe5.

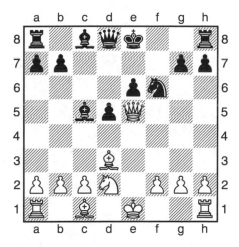

3) Black moves

Castling is the routine move, but an alert player will spot 1...♗xf2+. Black wins the f-pawn for nothing, as 2 ♔xf2 ♘g4+ costs White a queen.

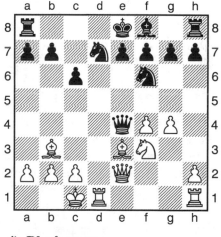

4) Black moves

1...♘xg4? leads to disaster: 2 ♗xf7+ ♔d8 (2...♔xf7 3 ♘g5+) 3 ♗b6+! and the discovered attack costs a queen after 3...axb6 4 ♕xe4.

TRICKY TACTIC 15   The Cunning Caro-Kann Trap

A stunning way to win a pawn

This trap is great. It uses the same basic idea as the previous Tricky Tactic, but with a classy little extra ingredient – a queen sacrifice! Over the years dozens of strong players – including masters – have fallen for this manoeuvre.

The piece and pawn structure normal for this trap commonly occurs via the Caro-Kann Defence. For this reason Black is usually the one springing the surprise.

Typical Position for the Caro-Kann Trap

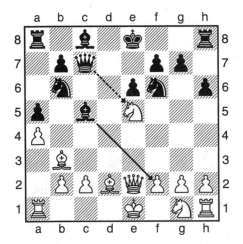

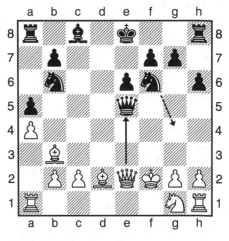

1a) Black moves

Black kicks off with 1...♗xf2+![1] 2 ♔xf2 (if 2 ♕xf2, then 2...♕xe5+) and now comes 2...♕xe5! (*1b*), offering a queen sacrifice.

1b) White moves

After 3 ♕xe5, the queen is regained by the knight fork 3...♘g4+. Next Black will capture with 4...♘xe5, ending up a pawn ahead.

---

1 Black **must play the moves in the right order!** 1...♕xe5 2 ♕xe5 ♗xf2+ would be a disaster as White doesn't have to capture the bishop (i.e. he plays 3 ♔f1) and remains a queen up.

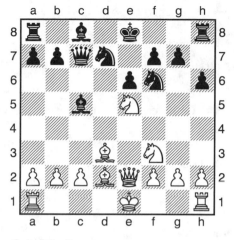

2a) Black moves

An innocent-looking Caro-Kann – but White is already trapped. Black begins 1...♘xe5 2 ♘xe5 (if 2 ♕xe5, then Black plays 2...♗xf2+) 2...♗xf2+ *(2b)*.

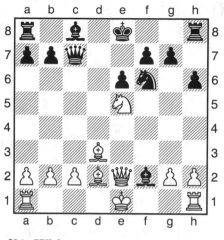

2b) White moves

The combination has won Black a pawn. If 3 ♕xf2, then 3...♕xe5+, while 3 ♔xf2 ♕xe5 4 ♕xe5 ♘g4+ forks king and queen.

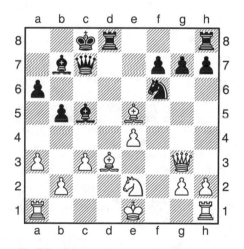

3) Black moves

The delightful 1...♗f2+! rescues a difficult game: 2 ♔xf2 ♕xe5 3 ♕xe5 ♘g4+ 4 ♔g3 ♘xe5 5 ♗c2 ♖d2 gives Black active play for the pawn.

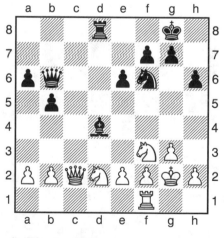

4) Black moves

A loosely related version too pretty not to give. 1...♗xf2! has the idea of 2 ♖xf2 ♘g4 with dual threats of 3...♕xf2+ and 3...♘e3+.

The ♗xf7+ and ♘e5+ Trick

Further fun on f7

By means of a decoy sacrifice, followed by a fork, White exploits an unwisely posted bishop on the g4-square.

The white bishop is first sacrificed for a pawn (as seen in Tricky Tactic 14). Again this serves to decoy the black king to the f7-square. This time, however, the subsequent knight fork takes place on the e5-square.

White generally wins a pawn.

Typical Position for the ♗xf7+ & ♘e5+ Trick

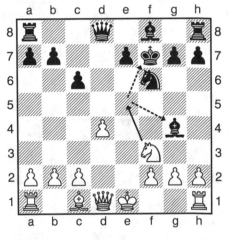

1a) White moves

The bishop sacrifice 1 ♗xf7+ forcibly decoys the black king onto a forking square after 1...♔xf7 (*1b*).

1b) White moves

After 2 ♘e5+ the black king and bishop fall victim to a knight fork. White wins a pawn; e.g., 2...♔g8 3 ♘xg4 ♘xg4 4 ♕xg4.

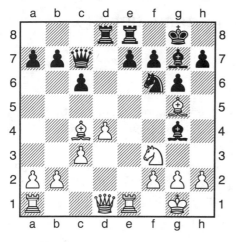

2a) White moves

Watch out if the e5-square is covered. Here the combination fails: 1 &xf7+? &xf7 2 &e5+ *(2b)*.

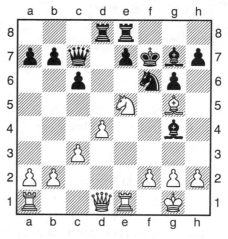

2b) Black moves

The queen capture 2...&xe5! wins Black a piece, since the white queen is also attacked: 3 &xe5 &xd1.

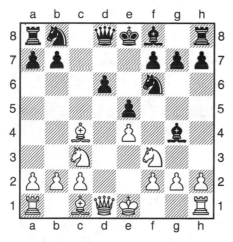

3) White moves

The e5-square is guarded, but, exceptionally, the tactic still works: 1 &xf7+ &xf7 2 &xe5+ and if 2...dxe5, then 3 &xd8.

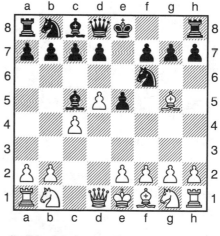

4) Black moves

Sometimes there is a choice of strong moves. Black has 1...&e4! (as well as 1...&xf2+), since if 2 &xd8?, 2...&xf2 is mate.

Pinning the Queen (1)

Fatal Attraction

This motif arises in early middlegame positions, where an opponent has castled kingside and moved the f-pawn. This leaves the king vulnerable to checks and pins along the diagonal.

If the enemy queen strays onto the diagonal, it is in severe risk of being pinned against its king by a bishop. The classic version is a knight sacrifice (or a knight swap) on the d5-square (d4 for Black). This attracts the queen to the fatal diagonal.

Typical Position for Pinning the Queen

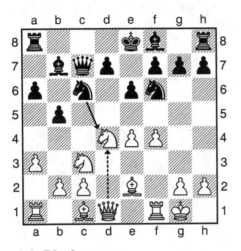

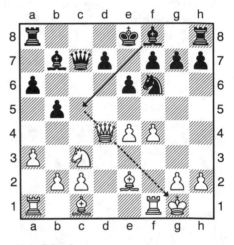

1a) Black moves

White's previous move (1 f4) was a terrible mistake. 1...♘xd4 lures the white queen onto the exposed diagonal after 2 ♕xd4 *(1b)*.

1b) Black moves

The white queen and king are sitting ducks, lined up on the a7-g1 diagonal. 2...♗c5 pins and wins the white queen.

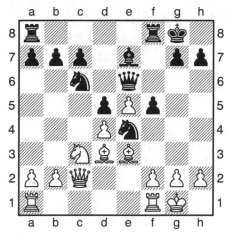

2a) White to move

A knight sacrifice serves both to open up the a2-g8 diagonal, and to lure the queen: 1 ♘xd5! ♛xd5 (2b).

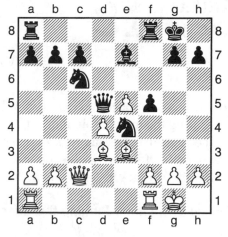

2b) White moves

Refusing the knight sacrifice would have left Black's game in ruins, but this is even worse. 2 ♗c4 wins the black queen.

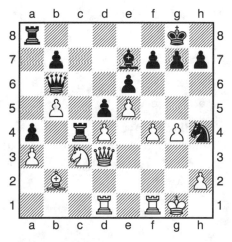

3) Black moves

A rook sacrifice for the d-pawn is less common, but can still do the business: 1...♖xd4 and then 2 ♛xd4 ♗c5 or 2 ♛e3 ♗c5.

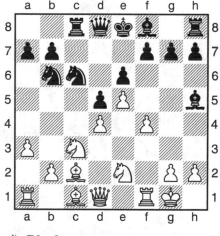

4) Black moves

The clever capture 1...♘xd4! neatly exploits both the h5-d1 pin (2 ♘xd4 ♗xd1) and the a7-g1 pin (2 ♛xd4 ♗c5).

Pinning the Queen (2)

Deadly decoys on d5

Following on from the previous Tricky Tactic, here are some more ways of winning material using the motif of pinning a queen on d5.

Of course, in these examples it is not compulsory for Black to recapture on d5 with the queen, falling for a deadly bishop pin. Declining the sacrifice will save the queen. But, as this leaves Black material down, the combination is successful regardless.

Typical Position for Pinning the Queen

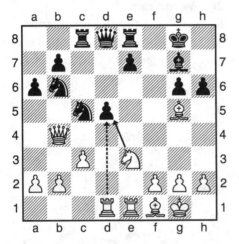

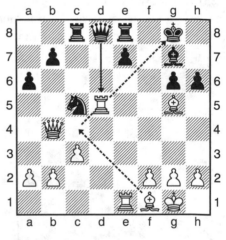

1a) White moves

The continuation 1 ♘xd5 ♘xd5 2 ♖xd5 (*1b*) – attacking Black's queen – gains White a pawn and a good position.

1b) Black moves

If Black captures the rook by 2...♕xd5, there would follow 3 ♗c4. The black queen is lost to a pin.

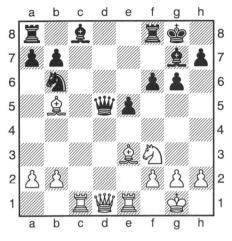

2) White moves

1 &c4! is a pretty win of the black queen: 1...&xc4 2 &xd5+ or 1...&xc4 2 &xc4.

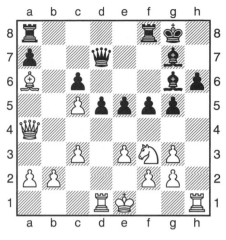

3) White moves

1 &xd5 exploits a pin on the black c-pawn (1...cxd5 2 &xd7), as well as the pin on the diagonal (1...&xd5 2 &c4).

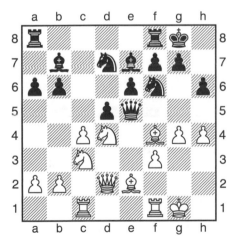

4) Black moves

It is worth noting this useful method of swapping queens. Black scoots out of trouble with 1...&xd4+ 2 &xd4 &c5.

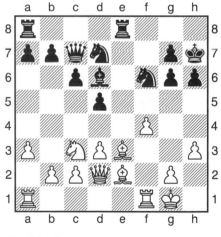

5) Black to move

Three motifs in one: 1...&xe3! (decoy) 2 &xe3 d4! (pawn fork and decoy) 3 &xd4 &c5 (pinning the queen). Superb.

The Zwischenzug

A big word for a brilliant trick

A *zwischenzug* is a forcing – and often unexpected – move played in the middle of a separate tactical sequence. It routinely occurs in the middle of a series of piece exchanges. Instead of making an (apparently) obligatory recapture, one side inserts a *zwischenzug* – usually a check and/or capture – to their advantage.

Zwischenzug is a German word that translates as an 'in-between move'. The theme is also sometimes called an intermezzo, or interpolation.

Typical Example of a Zwischenzug

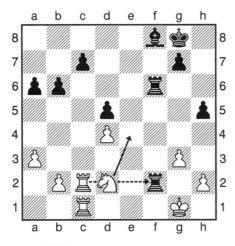 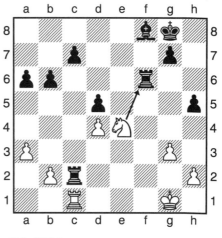

1a) White moves

The startling 1 ♘e4! (based on 1...dxe4 2 ♖xf2) is a fork. Black swaps rooks with 1...♖xc2 *(1b)*, planning to take the knight next move.

1b) White moves

Before recapturing the rook, White inserts the *zwischenzug* 2 ♘xf6+. After 2...gxf6 3 ♖xc2 White has won rook for bishop.

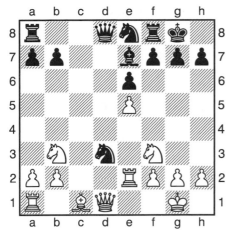

2a) Black moves

Many *zwischenzugs* involve a discovered attack. On 1...♘xe5! White must attend to his threatened queen, i.e. with 2 ♕xd8 *(2b)*.

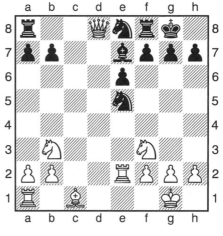

2b) Black moves

Before making a recapture on d8, Black inserts the in-between move 2...♘xf3+. After 3 gxf3 ♖xd8 Black is a pawn up.

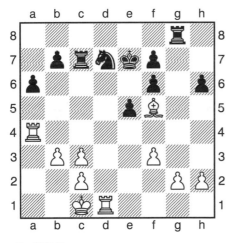

3) White moves

On 1 ♖c4! ♖xc4 White does not recapture immediately on c4. Inserting the *zwischenzug* 2 ♖xd7+ ♔e8 3 bxc4 wins a piece.

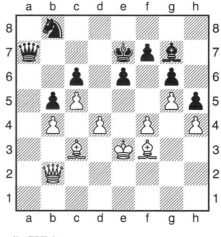

4) White moves

1 d5! ♗xc3 2 d6+ is a *zwischenzug* for positional gain: 2...♔d7 3 ♕xc3 establishes a mighty passed pawn on d6 for White.

More Knight Forks

Serve up several motifs

In games between experienced players, it is not likely someone will blunder and allow a straightforward knight fork. The key to creating a successful knight fork is to utilize other motifs in the combination as well – such as pins and sacrifices.

Decoy sacrifices can be highly effective in luring enemy major pieces onto squares vulnerable to a knight fork. This is especially so when the enemy king can be put in check as part of the combination.

Typical Knight Fork involving a Decoy

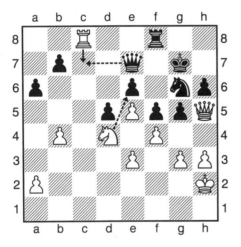

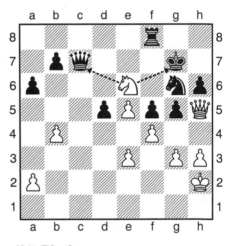

1a) White moves

1 ♖c7! is a sacrifice to force the black queen onto a disastrous square. After 1...♕xc7 White has the crushing 'Family Fork' 2 ♘xe6+ *(1b)*.

1b) Black moves

The black king, queen and rook are simultaneously attacked by White's knight. As Black must move out of check, the queen is lost.

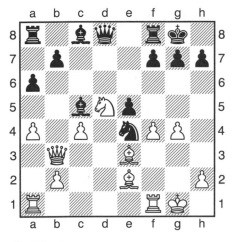

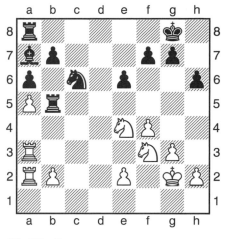

2) Black moves

The easily-missed 1...♘d2 uses a pin to achieve a fork. After 2 ♕d3 ♗xe3+ 3 ♕xe3 ♘xf1 Black has won rook for knight.

3) Black moves

1...♘b4 wins material, as White's attacked rook on a2 has just one retreat square. 2 ♖a1 ♘c2 forks both white rooks.

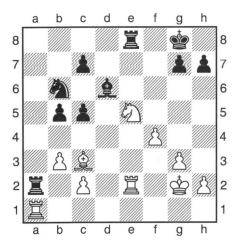

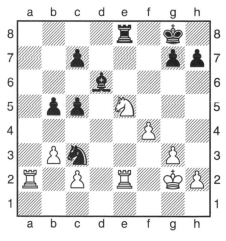

4a) Black moves

This elegant combination was played by former World Champion Boris Spassky in 2002: 1...♘d5! 2 ♖xa2 ♘xc3 (4b).

4b) White moves

Wonderful – the two rooks are well and truly forked. White loses a full rook back, and ends up a piece down.

A sneaky surprise on c7

Inexperienced players often fall for this one. It occurs if Black has failed to castle quickly, and a white knight is able to invade the c7-square. The knight checks the king on e8, attacking the rook on a8 at the same time.

Unless White has sacrificed to set up the tactic, this knight fork wins material. Adding insult to injury, Black's king has to move in response to the knight check, and is left poorly placed in the centre.

Typical Position for the Knight Fork

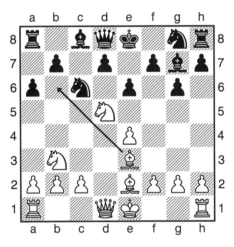 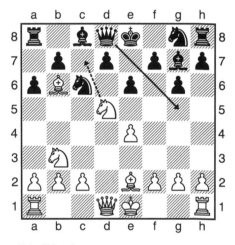

1a) White moves

Instead of retreating his attacked knight from the d5-square, White counter-attacks. 1 ♗b6 *(1b)* threatens the black queen.

1b) Black moves

The queen must move (i.e. 1...♕g5 or 1...♕h4). White continues with the knight fork 2 ♘c7+, winning the rook on a8.

54

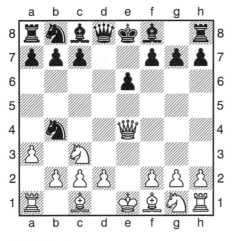

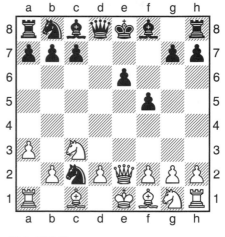

2a) Black moves

The pawn advance 1...f5! is anti-positional, but effective. White's queen is driven from the defence of the c2-square; e.g., 2 ♕e2 ♘xc2+ *(2b)*.

2b) White moves

The white king must move out of check. After 3 ♔d1 ♘xa1 Black has won a rook and a pawn – an easy win.

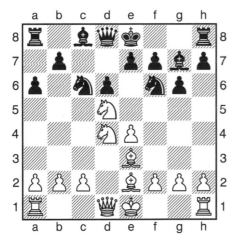

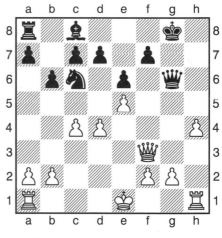

3) White moves

1 ♘xc6 bxc6 2 ♗b6 spells disaster for Black right in the opening: 2...♕d7 3 ♘c7+ forks the black king and rook.

4) Black moves

The well-calculated 1...♘xd4! sets up a winning ...♘c2+ fork next move. 2 ♕xa8 fails to the mating attack 2...♕d3! 3 ♕xc8+ ♔g7.

The ♗xh7+ Queen Fork

Harvesting h-pawns

It is remarkable how many victims this trap claims each year. Watch out for positions where White has the possibility of a temporary bishop sacrifice (♗xh7+), forcing Black to capture on h7 with the king.

In such circumstances, any unprotected black piece (typically a bishop or a knight) risks succumbing to a white queen fork. The queen checks on either the h5-square, or somewhere on the b1-h7 diagonal. Typically White regains his sacrificed piece and ends up an h-pawn ahead.

Typical Position for ♗xh7+ followed by ♕h5+

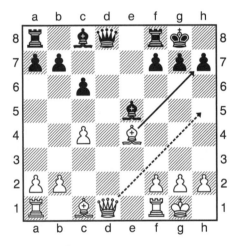

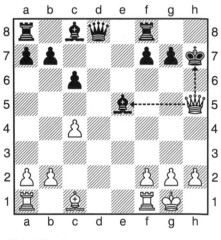

1a) White moves

The unguarded black bishop on e5 allows White to sacrifice with 1 ♗xh7+ (if 1 ♕h5, then 1...f5 defends). On 1...♚xh7 comes 2 ♕h5+ *(1b)*.

1b) Black moves

The black king and bishop are forked. After 2...♚g8 3 ♕xe5 White has regained the piece, and won a pawn.

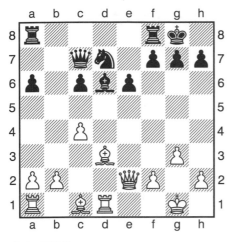

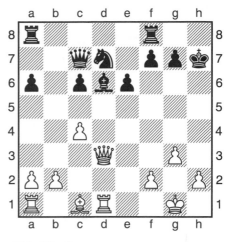

2a) White moves

Here the queen check comes on the b1-h7 diagonal, following 1 ♗xh7+ ♔xh7 2 ♕d3+ *(2b)*.

2b) Black moves

Black is forked – his king and bishop are both attacked. Next White plays 3 ♕xd6, regaining a bishop and winning a pawn.

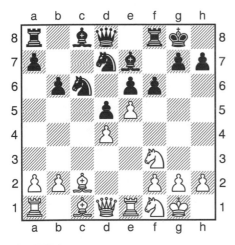

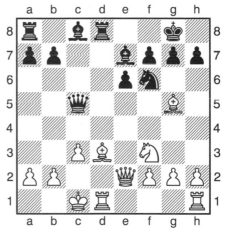

3) White moves

Here the c2-square is utilized for the fork. 1 ♗xh7+ ♔xh7 2 ♕c2+ targets the loose black knight on c6.

4) White moves

A deep version: 1 ♗xf6 ♗xf6 2 ♗xh7+! ♔xh7 3 ♖xd8 ♗xd8 4 ♕d3+ regaining the bishop with an advantage; e.g., 4...g6 5 ♕xd8.

Clearance Sacrifices

Making way for the winner

Occasionally a position arises where a combination would be possible – but one of the attacking side's own pieces is actually in the way. If the potential combination is extremely strong, it can be worth the attacker playing a forcing sacrifice of his own piece, just to clear lines for his other pieces.

These pretty clearance sacrifices can easily be missed by the defender. This is because the initial move is often surprising – as it is not really related to the combination. The sole purpose is to jettison the piece that is blocking lines, allowing the real combination to follow.

Typical Position for a Clearance Sacrifice

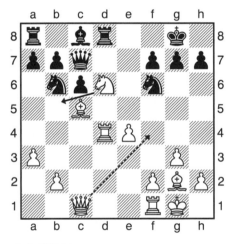

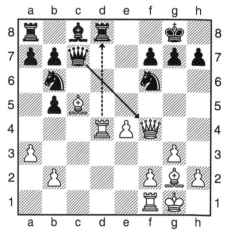

1a) White moves

If the white knight on d6 were absent, a winning combination would be possible. White plays the stunning sacrifice 1 ♘b5!! cxb5 2 ♕f4 *(1b)*.

1b) Black moves

The black queen is overloaded (1...♕xf4 2 ♖xd8+) and White wins. The purpose of White's knight sacrifice was to clear the diagonal between f4 and c7 and the line between d4 and d8.

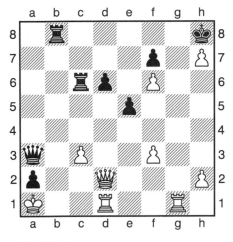

2a) Black moves

Annoyingly, the black a-pawn provides shelter for the white king. Black jettisons it with 1...♖b1+ 2 ♖xb1 axb1♕++ 3 ♔xb1 *(2b)*.

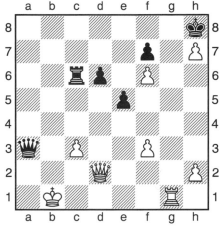

2b) Black moves

Now attacking lines are opened, and the white king is doomed. 1...♖b6+ 2 ♔c2 ♖b2+ wins easily.

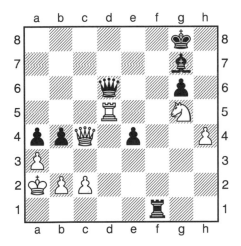

3a) Black moves

1...b3+! is a fine sacrifice that also blocks a defence by the white queen. The point is revealed after 2 cxb3 ♖a1+! *(3b)*.

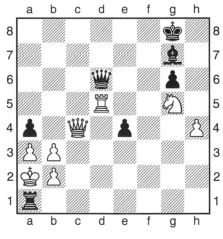

3b) White moves

This *rook decoy sacrifice* mates: 3 ♔xa1 ♕xa3+ 4 ♔b1 ♕xb2. Note how Black's initial sacrifice (1...b3+) *cleared the diagonal for his queen.*

TRICKY TACTIC 24

Desperado Sacrifices

Sell yourself dearly

A 'desperado'[1] occurs when a piece or pawn – about to be captured – inflicts as much damage as possible before departing the chessboard. This can occur because a piece is trapped, but usually a desperado occurs during a series of piece exchanges.

If a piece is inevitably going to be swapped off, sometimes it is possible to insert a surprise capture – often with check – to win material.

Typical Position for a Desperado

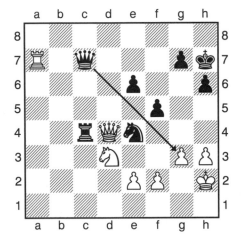

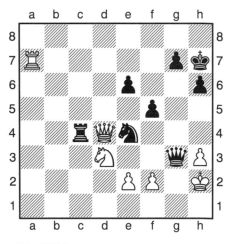

1a) Black moves

An exchange of queens is inevitable. But instead of a routine swap (1...♖xd4 2 ♖xc7) Black plays the 'desperado' move 1...♕xg3+ *(1b)*.

1b) White moves

After 2 fxg3 ♖xd4 Black has won a pawn. Queens have still been exchanged, but the black queen successfully sold itself for a cost.

---

1 There is also a second definition of a *desperado*, being a piece that tries to sacrifice itself repeatedly to bring about a stalemate. This theme is seen in Tricky Tactics 27-29 (Rampant Rooks and Kamikaze Queens).

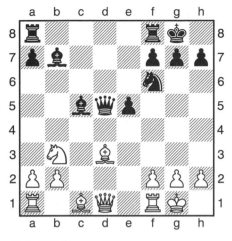

2a) White moves

The combination 1 ♗xh7+ ♔xh7 2 ♕xd5 *(2b)* seems to win a pawn for White (since if 2...♗xd5 or 2...♘xd5 there comes the capture 3 ♘xc5).

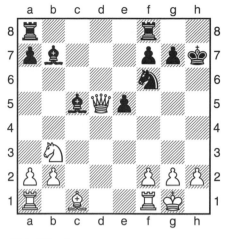

2b) Black moves

However 2...♗xf2+! is a useful desperado, as the black bishop on c5 is lost anyway. Black keeps material equality: 3 ♖xf2 ♘xd5.

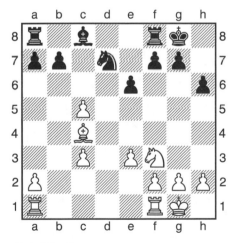

3a) White moves

A modest positional desperado. Black aims to regain his pawn with advantage (by 1...♘xc5) so White continues 1 c6 *(3b)*.

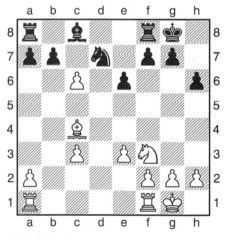

3b) Black moves

After 1...bxc6 Black's pawn-structure is weakened. The white c5-pawn could not be saved, but did inflict damage before departing.

TRICKY TACTIC 25

Stalemates

If you snooze you lose... or maybe draw

The concept of stalemate can seem bizarre. A player, losing horribly, is able to swindle a half-point by leaving himself with no legal moves. Scandalous! Whatever the justice of this, stalemates can very occasionally be a fantastic way to salvage a draw.

Stalemates mostly occur in endgames where material is greatly reduced. The defending side often attempts to sacrifice a last piece to bring about a stalemate position. In most cases this devious scheme is preventable – except if an opponent forgets about stalemate as a possibility.

Sometimes beautiful stalemates remain well hidden until the trap is sprung. So, winning or losing, stay awake!

Typical Position for a Stalemate

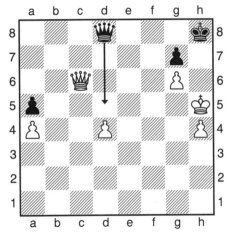

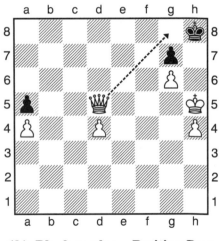

1a) Black moves

Two pawns down, Black looks in trouble. There follows the unexpected queen sacrifice 1...♛d5+, forcing 2 ♕xd5 *(1b)*.

1b) Black to play – Position Drawn

White's queen now unwillingly covers the g8-square, and Black's king has no legal moves. The game is a draw by stalemate.

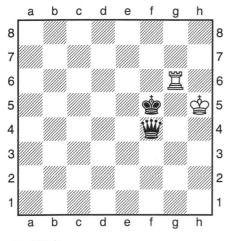

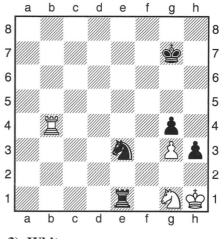

2) White moves

A rook for queen down, White saves half a point with 1 ♖f6+. After 1...♔xf6 White is stalemated.

3) White moves

A pretty stalemate materializes after 1 ♖xg4+! ♘xg4. White has no legal moves and is not in check – so draw.

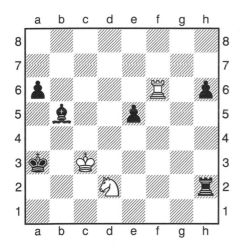

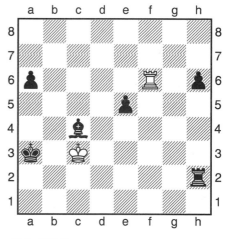

4a) White moves

A well-disguised example. After 1 ♘c4+ Black blundered with 1...♗xc4? *(4b)*, having assumed that White would simply recapture.

4b) White moves

Big mistake! The rook sacrifice 2 ♖xa6+! ♗xa6 left the white king stalemated, and so the game was drawn.

Rook Endgame Stalemates

Rooked out of half a point

There are a few startling stalemate tricks that can arise in simple rook and pawn endings. For some reason even experienced players can miss the danger. Perhaps these oversights are not specific to rook endings, but are typical of stalemates in general. After a whole game spent trying to gain material, it is easy to forget that suddenly one side might start giving up pieces on purpose!

The usual rook endgame stalemate is short and sweet. In an inferior position, the defender uses his rook to capture what appears to be a defended pawn. Although the rook is lost, an immediate stalemate results.

Typical Position for a Rook Endgame Stalemate

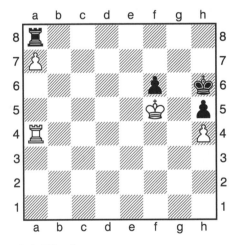

1a) Black moves

The capture 1...♜xa7 saves an otherwise lost endgame, even though White can take the black rook with 2 ♖xa7 *(1b)*.

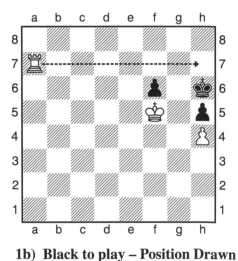

1b) Black to play – Position Drawn

Although White is a rook ahead, the game is drawn by stalemate. Black is not in check, but has no legal moves.

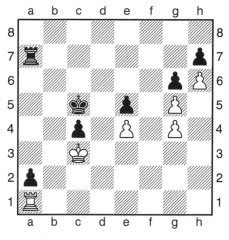

2) White moves

The saving resource is 1 ♖xa2. The recapture 1...♖xa2 by Black gives a draw by stalemate.

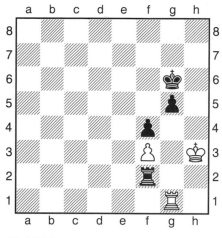

3) White moves

The white f-pawn appears doomed, but there is a standard saving device: 1 ♖xg5+. If 1...♔xg5 White is stalemated.

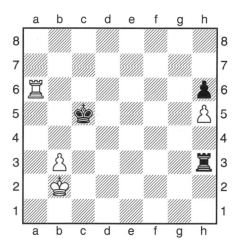

4a) Black moves

A world-class grandmaster overlooked a sneaky opportunity to draw here. 1...♖xh5! 'falls' for the skewer 2 ♖a5+ ♔b4 *(4b)*.

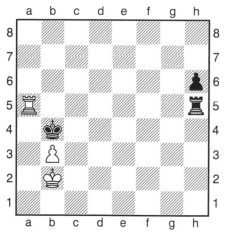

4b) White moves

The black rook can be captured for free with 3 ♖xh5 – but then the black king is left stalemated.

TRICKY TACTIC 27

The Rampant Rook

A stalemate save by a suicidal rook

A rook that repeatedly checks the enemy king – even if the rook can be captured every move – is known as a Rampant Rook. These positions can be great fun, as the king runs all over the board pursued by the crazy rook!

Rampant Rook positions typically arise in the endgame when:

a) The defender is happy with a draw;

b) The defender is in stalemate except for being able to move his rook.

If the rook can sacrifice itself, a draw by stalemate results. It is vital that the opponent's king cannot escape the checks, and that the stalemate structure is not disturbed in the course of administering the checks.

Typical Position for the Rampant Rook

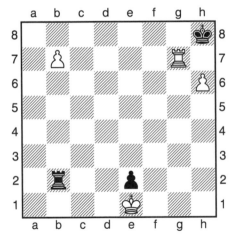

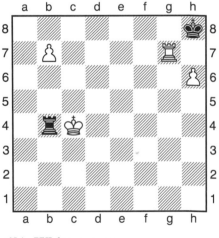

1a) Black moves

The black king is hemmed in by the white rook on g7. Black jettisons material with 1...♖b1+ 2 ♔xe2 ♖b2+ 3 ♔d3 ♖b3+ 4 ♔c4 ♖b4+! *(1b)*.

1b) White moves

If White captures the rook, Black is stalemated. Otherwise the Rampant Rook checks forever: 5 ♔c5 ♖b5+! 6 ♔c6 ♖b6+! 7 ♔c7 ♖xb7+!.

66

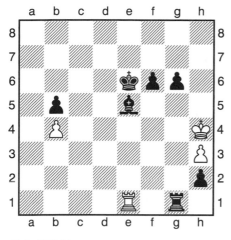

2a) White moves

1 ♖xe5+! saves the game. A recapture is stalemate, and otherwise the checks begin; e.g., 1...♔d6 2 ♖d5+ ♔c6 3 ♖c5+ ♔b6 *(2b)*.

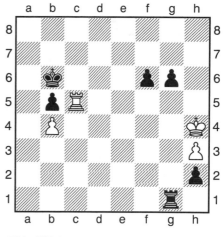

2b) White moves

4 ♖c6+! draws. Not 4 ♖xb5+? ♔c6! 5 ♖c5+ ♔d6 6 ♖d5+ ♔xd5! when the b-pawn can move, so no stalemate arises.

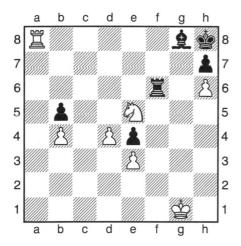

3a) Black moves

Shock the grandmaster! In a simul against Maurice Ashley, Berkeley student Aviv Adler found 1...♖f1+! 2 ♔g2 ♖g1+ 3 ♔f2 ♖g2+ 4 ♔e1 ♖e2+ *(3b)*.

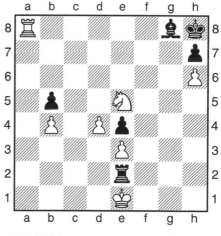

3b) White moves

The rook repeatedly offers itself, since a white capture causes stalemate. 5 ♔d1 ♖d2+ 6 ♔c1 ♖c2+ 7 ♔b1 ♖b2+ 8 ♔a1 ♖b1+! draws.

The surreal world of the stalemate

This motif is similar to that of the previous Tricky Tactic, the *Rampant Rook*. Once again, the defender's king is in a stalemate position. Here the aim is to force a draw by repeatedly trying to sacrifice the queen with check. Compared with a rook – where dozens of checks are sometimes made – the power of the queen means the Kamikaze effect is achieved far quicker.

A Kamikaze Queen can be a miraculous last chance to draw from an abysmal position. But care is needed about the checking squares. It is vital not to disrupt the stalemate formation.

Typical Position for a Kamikaze Queen

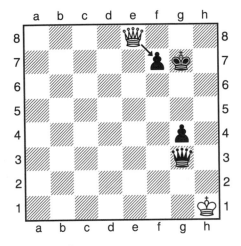

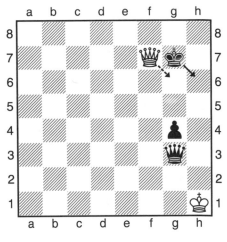

1a) White moves

Two pawns down, White's saviour is the black queen, poorly positioned so that it stalemates the white king. To draw, White sacrifices his own queen with 1 ♕xf7+ *(1b)*.

1b) Black moves

The draw is now inevitable, as 1...♚xf7 leaves White stalemated. If Black tries 1...♚h6, White can continue 2 ♕g6+, forcing Black to take the queen.

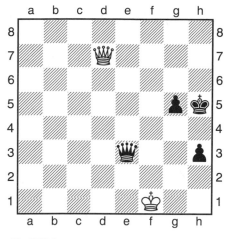

2) White moves

Black (a grandmaster) had just pushed his pawn to h3. This error allows 1 ♕g4+ ♔h6 (1...♔xg4 is stalemate) 2 ♕h5+ and the queen keeps checking.

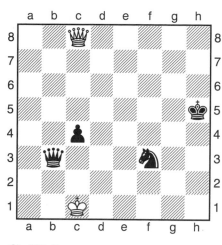

3) White moves

Another high-level game where Black unwittingly created a stalemate net. 1 ♕g4+ ♔h6 2 ♕g6+ ♔xg6 is a draw, despite Black's extra queen, knight and pawn.

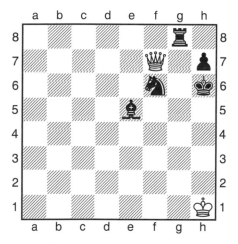

4a) White moves

White must choose kamikaze squares carefully (the stalemate vanishes after 1 ♕g6+? ♔xg6 or 1...hxg6): e.g., 1 ♕xh7+! ♔g5 2 ♕h4+ ♔f5 3 ♕e4+! *(4b)*.

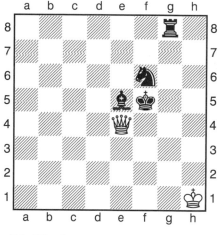

4b) Black moves

A picturesque situation. Black can capture the queen (drawing by stalemate) or run with the king, and face perpetual checks, i.e. 3...♔e6 4 ♕d5+.

29 Kamikaze Queen *and* Rampant Rook

It's chess, Jim, but not as we know it

You are now entering the twilight zone, where the normal laws of chess are suspended. Around you, Kamikaze Queens and Rampant Rooks embark on suicidal missions with abandon, and draws occur despite a huge material disparity between the players.

It must be admitted that positions where both a rook and a queen are sacrificed to force stalemate are exceptional. Rarer still are those remarkable positions where two rooks and a queen are given up. But what this motif lacks in quantity, it makes up for in quality. These combinations are always stunning.

Typical Position for a Kamikaze Queen & Rook

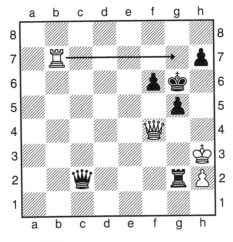

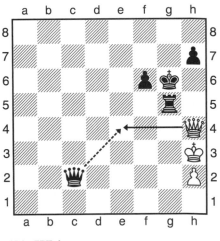

1a) White moves

On 1 ♖g7+ (heading for 1...♔xg7 2 ♕xf6+! ♔xf6 stalemate) Black declines the rook with 1...♔h5, but White re-sacrifices: 2 ♖xg5+ ♖xg5 3 ♕h4+ ♔g6 (*1b*).

1b) White moves

An altered stalemate structure – White's king now has the flight square h4 – is often disastrous. But with 4 ♕e4+! ♕xe4 the draw is achieved.

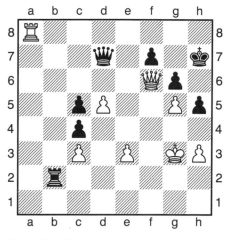

2a) Black moves

Facing mate threats, Black's amazing defence involves sacrificing first a pawn and then his rook: 1...h4+! 2 ♔xh4 ♖b8! *(2b)*.

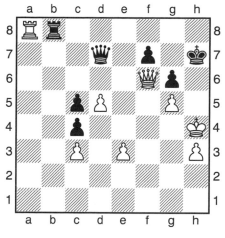

2b) White moves

On 3 ♖xb8 Black's queen is also thrown into the pot. By 3...♕xh3+ (also 3...♕g4+) 4 ♔xh3 Black achieves the desired draw by stalemate.

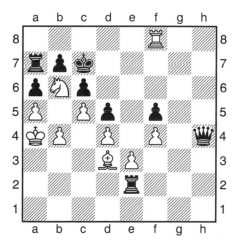

3a) Black moves

Black lost this game, believing checkmate on c8 was unstoppable. The missed defence was 1...♖a8!! 2 ♖xa8 (2 ♘xa8+ ♔d7) 2...♖a2+ 3 ♔b3 ♖b2+ *(3b)*.

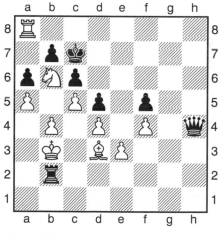

3b) White moves

On 4 ♔xb2 ♕f2+ the two sacrificed rooks are followed by a kamikaze queen: 5 ♔b3 ♕b2+ 6 ♔xb2 stalemate. Out of this world...

71

The ♘g5 & ♗xb7 Trap

The Discovery of the Century

Over the past hundred years, countless pieces have been lost to this manoeuvre. Not too long ago a world-class grandmaster somehow fell into our basic version (below). I won't say who it was, or Mickey Adams will never talk to me again.

The trap uses a *discovered attack* against a black bishop on b7. White plays ♘g5 in a position where checkmate on h7 is threatened (because the white queen is located on the b1-h7 diagonal).

It doesn't matter if the white knight on g5 is captured. White captures the black bishop, and can sometimes win the black queen's rook as well.

Typical Position for the ♘g5 & ♗xb7 Trap

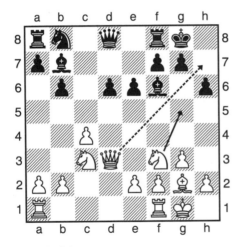 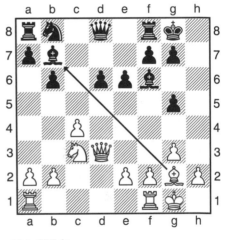

1a) White moves

The knight sacrifice 1 ♘g5 has two threats: a discovered attack on b7, and mate with ♕h7. To avoid mate Black captures with 1...hxg5 *(1b)*.

1b) White moves

With 2 ♗xb7 White achieves more than a trade of knight for bishop. The black rook on a8 is trapped, and will be lost next move.

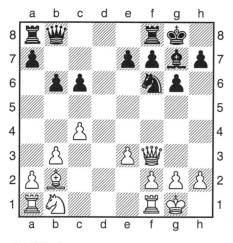

2) Black moves

1...♘g4 wins material. White must deal with the threat of ...♕xh2 mate, but after 2 ♕xg4 ♗xb2 the white rook is trapped.

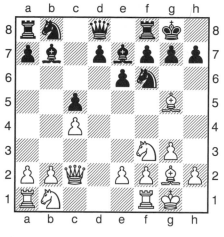

3) White moves

This concealed version runs 1 ♗xf6 ♗xf6 2 ♘g5! ♗xg5 3 ♗xb7 and White wins rook for bishop after 3...♘c6 4 ♗xa8.

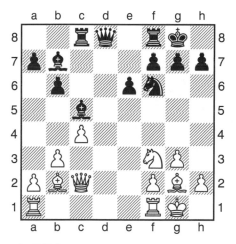

4) White moves

Here 1 ♘g5 wins outright (i.e. 1...g6 2 ♗xb7). The vicious point is that 1...♗xg2 2 ♗xf6! creates the mate threat 3 ♕xh7.

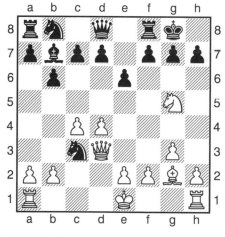

5) Black moves

A defensive resource: Black returns material with 1...♘e4!?, though White keeps an edge with 2 ♗xe4 ♗xe4 3 ♕xe4 ♕xg5 4 ♕xa8.

The Deadly d-File Discovery

Don't dally on d4

This version of a *discovered attack* continues to trap naïve souls who place their queens in vulnerable positions on the d-file.

The scheme is simple: an attack on the exposed enemy queen is unveiled, by moving a bishop out of the way with check. Often this requires the bishop to be sacrificed – hardly an issue when a queen is won in return.

Typical Position for the Deadly d-file Discovery

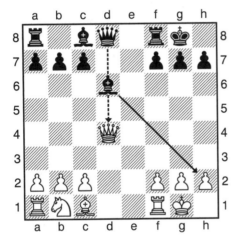

1a) Black moves

The bishop sacrifice 1...♗xh2+ *(1b)* clears a path along the d-file. This produces a discovered attack on the undefended white queen.

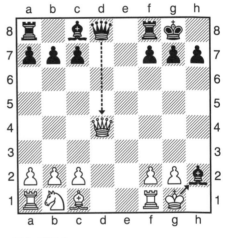

1b) White moves

As it is check, White captures with 2 ♔xh2. After 2...♕xd4, Black has won a queen for just a bishop.

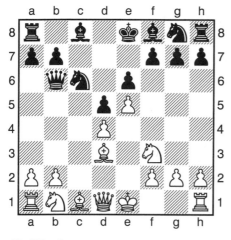

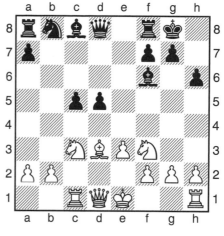

2) Black moves

Snatching the d-pawn is a fatal but common error: 1...♘xd4? 2 ♘xd4 ♛xd4 3 ♗b5+! and White wins the black queen on d4.

3) White moves

Here White uses the trap to win the d-pawn with 1 ♘xd5!, since on 1...♛xd5? would come 2 ♗h7+ ♔xh7 3 ♛xd5.

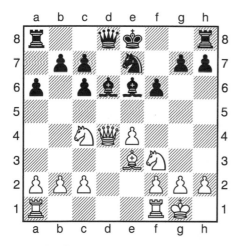

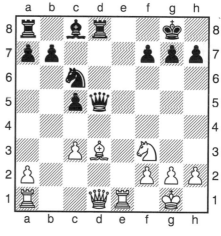

4) Black moves

The white queen is protected, but a loose knight on c4 still costs a pawn: 1...♗xh2+! 2 ♔xh2 ♛xd4 3 ♘xd4 ♗xc4.

5) White to move

The flashy rook sacrifice 1 ♖e8+! deflects a key defender of the black queen. White wins after 1...♖xe8 2 ♗xh7+ ♔xh7 3 ♛xd5.

The Old ♘d5 Trick (1)

Angle an attack on a5

This motif appears where the black queen has been developed to the a5-square, and White has a queen on d2 and a knight on c3. In such positions, the move ♘d5 by White frequently creates a useful discovered attack on the black queen. The knight move can be possible even when the d5-square is well guarded.

White is ostensibly offering a queen exchange, but no ordinary one. With Black's king on the g8-square, the plan is to insert a cheeky *zwischenzug* (in-between move). The white knight aims to snap off an undefended piece or pawn on e7 with check.

Typical Position for the ♘d5 Discovered Attack

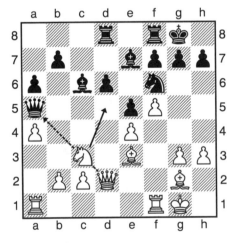

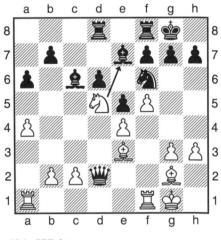

1a) White moves

1 ♘d5 unveils a discovered attack on Black's queen (from the white queen). A swap with 1...♛xd2 (*1b*) is forced, but now comes the *zwischenzug*.

1b) White moves

White inserts 2 ♘xe7+!, a capture with check. Only after 2...♔h8 does White recapture the queen with 3 ♗xd2 – having won a bishop.

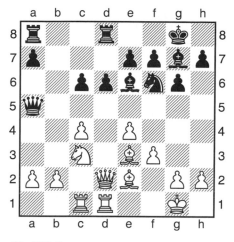

2) White moves

Here 1 ♘d5 is possible, but does not win *as Black's king has access to f8.* 1...♕xd2 2 ♘xc7+? (2 ♘xf6+) 2...♔f8! would win a piece for Black.

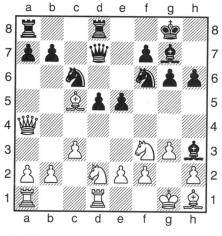

3) Black moves

A lethal mating version to beware of: 1...♘d4! and the white queen is lost. Black threatens ...♕xa4, and if 2 ♕xd7, 2...♘xe2 is checkmate.

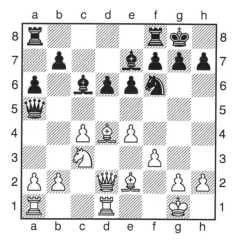

4a) White moves

Sometimes Black answers 1 ♘d5 with 1...♕d8. Nevertheless, White often gains an advantage, i.e. here with 2 ♗b6 *(4b)*.

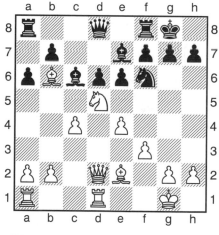

4b) Black moves

Following 2...♕d7 3 ♘xe7+ ♕xe7 4 ♕xd6 White has an extra pawn and a great position.

The Old ♘d5 Trick (2)

Advanced versions

A discovered attack can enable seemingly impossible moves to be made. As with the previous Tricky Tactic, White's knight leaps with impunity onto the d5-square. The advance can occur regardless of how well the square is protected by enemy pieces and pawns.

Before thinking of capturing the knight, Black must attend to his own undefended queen on a5. By then it is too late. The white knight has moved swiftly on, often collecting a stray piece or pawn by means of a *zwischenzug*.

Typical Position for the ♘d5 Discovered Attack

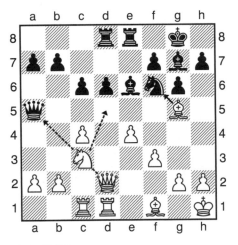

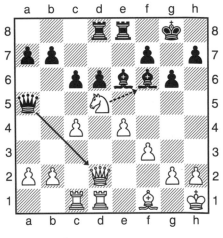

1a) White moves

1 ♗xf6 ♗xf6 2 ♘d5! *(1b)* sets up the *zwischenzug* on the f6-square. Black has no time to capture the knight, as the queen is under attack.

1b) Black moves

After 2...♕xd2 3 ♘xf6+! White wins a piece (i.e. 3...♔h8 4 ♖xd2). Note 3...♔g7 fails to the further *zwischenzug* 4 ♘xe8+.

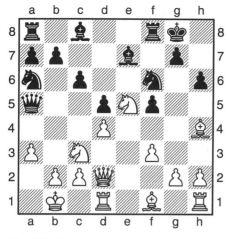

2) White moves

1 ♘xd5! wins the house (if 1...♕xd2, 2 ♘xe7+). Particularly aesthetic is the line 1...♕xd5 2 ♗c4 pinning Black's queen.

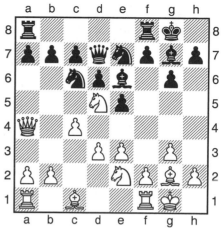

3) Black moves

In this routine version, Black seeks only to free his game: 1...♘xd5! 2 cxd5 ♘d4! 3 ♕d1 ♘xe2+ 4 ♕xe2 ♗h3.

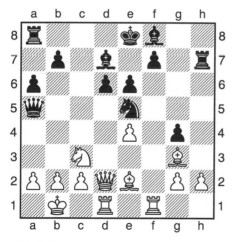

4a) White moves

The high-level game Firman-Galliamova, Moscow 2002 saw White proceed 1 ♘d5! ♕xd2 2 ♘f6+ ♔e7 3 ♖xd2 *(4b)*.

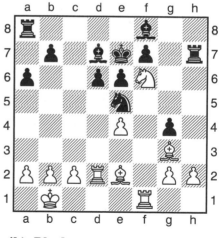

4b) Black moves

There is no defence! White has two powerful threats: 4 ♘xh7 and 4 ♗xe5 dxe5 5 ♖xd7 mate.

The Old ♘d5 Trick (3)

Central pawns for free

This trap uses similar principles to the two previous Tricky Tactics, but here the opposing queens are situated on an open c-file. As before, the white knight on c3 moves to create a discovered attack on Black's queen.

That said, the *modus operandi* tends to be slightly different. White usually uses the knight discovery to capture an apparently well-protected enemy pawn (either on e4 and d5). A *zwischenzug* is then used to swap the knight off next move, right in the middle of Black's queen exchange.

Typical Position for the ♘d5 Discovered Attack

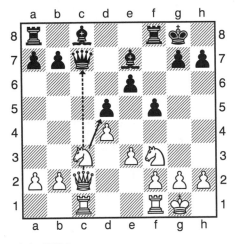

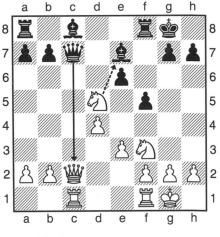

1a) White moves

The surprise capture 1 ♘xd5! *(1b)* is possible as Black must attend to his undefended queen (if 1...exd5?, 2 ♕xc7).

1b) Black moves

On 1...♕xc2 (intending 2 ♖xc2 exd5), White can play the 'in-between-move' 2 ♘xe7+. Black ends up a pawn down after 2...♔f7 3 ♖xc2 ♔xe7.

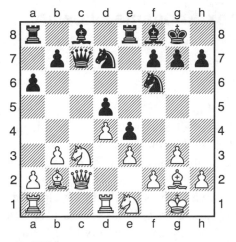

2) White moves

This example (played by Grandmaster Tony Miles) shows how to snatch an e-pawn for free: 1 ♘xe4! ♕xc2 2 ♘xf6+ ♘xf6 3 ♘xc2.

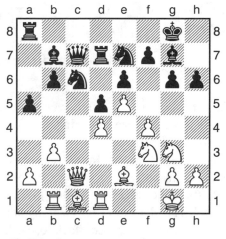

3) Black moves

Even the most well-protected pawn can be humbled by a *zwischenzug*: 1...♘xe5! 2 ♕xc7 ♘xf3+ does the trick.

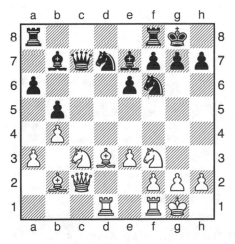

4a) White moves

The remarkable 1 ♘d5!! is good, even though Black replies 1...♘xd5, defending his queen. There follows 2 ♗xh7+ ♚h8 (*4b*).

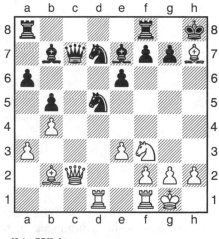

4b) White moves

After 3 ♕xc7 ♘xc7 4 ♖xd7 the rook on the seventh rank attacks various black pieces. White will emerge a pawn ahead.

The Rook Endgame Skewer

What a difference a square makes

This sneaky trap will catch even the odd forgetful master. It occurs in rook endgames, where a white pawn is nearing promotion, and the black king is on the other side of the board. Black assumes – because his rook is well posted behind the passed pawn – everything is under control. In fact, a precise placement of the black king is critical, or Black can lose instantly.

In the generic version (below), the *only* defensive squares for the black king are g7 and h7. The black king *must* occupy one of these squares once White's pawn advances to the seventh rank, or else Black loses. A king on other squares – namely f7, e7 and d7 – allows White the deadly skewer.

Typical Position for the Rook Endgame Skewer

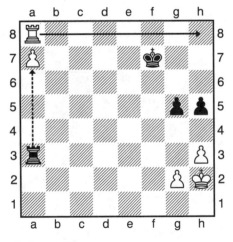

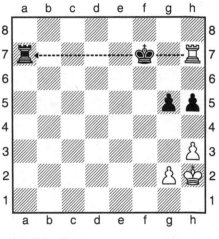

1a) White moves

The black king is on the wrong square. 1 ♖h8! threatens the winning pawn promotion a8♕. There follows 1...♖xa7 2 ♖h7+! *(1b)*.

1b) Black moves

The pawn has been captured – but Black's king and rook are skewered. Once Black moves out of check, 3 ♖xa7 wins for White.

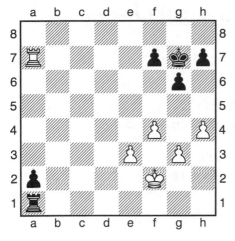

2) White moves

To defend against a ...♖h1 skewer, White *must* play 1 ♔g2 – the only move to draw. Note that 1 ♔f3? fails to 1...♖f1+ and next 2...a1♕.

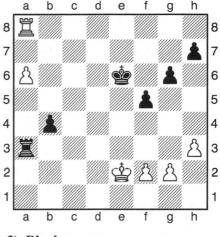

3) Black moves

The pawn advance 1 a7 wins. Black's king can't hide from a rook check, since 1...♔f7, 1...♔e7 and 1...♔d7 all fail to the 2 ♖h8 skewer.

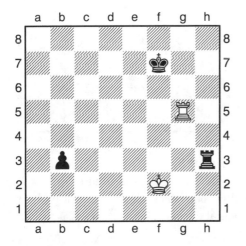

4a) Black moves

From Minasian-Navara, Bled Olympiad 2002. If 1...b2, 2 ♖g1 draws, so instead came 1...♖h1! *(4b)*, preparing to advance the b-pawn.

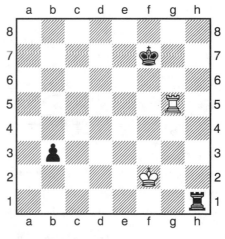

4b) White moves

White has no defence! On 2 ♖b5 (if 2 ♔g2, then 2...b2) comes 2...b2! 3 ♖xb2 ♖h2+ skewering the white king and rook.

Perpetual Checks

Bailing out to a draw

A draw by perpetual occurs when one side repeatedly checks the opponent's king, move after move. It is not checkmate – the king can move out of check each time – but the checks can never be stopped.

Experienced players use perpetuals to bail out of dubious positions. If the enemy king must be stripped of pawn cover to allow the checks to begin, then brute force is used to achieve this. Other versions are subtler, and can involve pretty decoys or deflections.

Queens are excellent at giving perpetuals, even in the middlegame.

Typical Position for a Perpetual Check

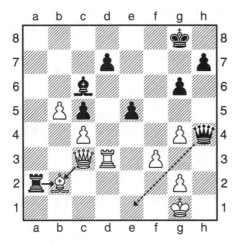

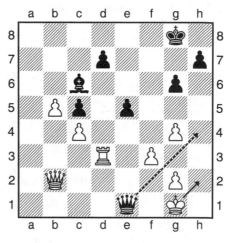

1a) Black moves

In a poor position, Black deflects the white queen with 1...♖xb2. After 2 ♕xb2 the black queen can penetrate by 2...♕e1+ *(1b)*.

1b) White moves

There is an escape square for the white king, but Black can force a draw by perpetual check: 3 ♔h2 ♕h4+ 4 ♔g1 ♕e1+.

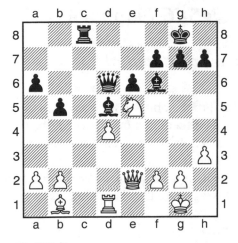

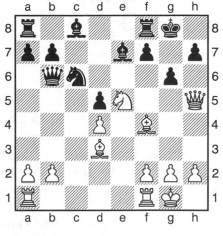

2) White moves

Not liking his position, White forces a draw with 1 ♗xh7+ ♚xh7 2 ♕h5+ ♚g8 3 ♕xf7+ ♚h7 4 ♕h5+ ♚g8, etc.

3) White moves

Two pieces are sacrificed to remove the defending pawn-cover: 1 ♘xg6 hxg6 2 ♗xg6 fxg6 3 ♕xg6+ ♚h8 4 ♕h6+ ♚g8 5 ♕g6+, etc.

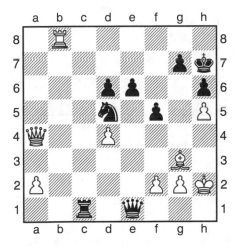

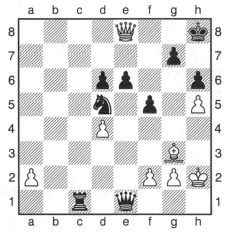

4a) White moves

Things look grim for White (mate on h1 is threatened), but the pawn on h5 assists in a neat save: 1 ♖h8+! ♚xh8 2 ♕e8+ *(4b)*.

4b) Black moves

The idea of White's rook decoy sacrifice is revealed. 2...♚h7 3 ♕g6+ ♚g8 4 ♕e8+ ♚h7 5 ♕g6+ is a draw by perpetual check.

The ♕g5-f6 Perpetual

A sacrifice on g7 comes as standard

This drawing tactic normally features a sacrifice of rook or bishop for a pawn on the g7-square, exposing the castled black king. Black has little option but to accept the sacrifice. White's queen can then swoop into the g5-square, with check, and administer a perpetual by checking alternately on the squares g5 and f6.

A point to note is that the black rook needs to be in its usual castled position. This prevents f8 from being a flight square for the black king, once the checks begin.

Typical Position for the ♕g5-f6 Perpetual Check

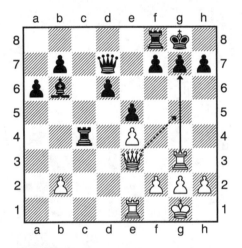

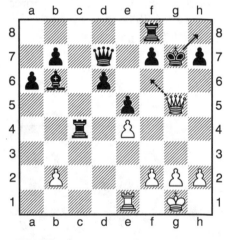

1a) White moves

A recapture on b6 would leave White two pawns down. Instead 1 ♖xg7+! ♔xg7 (if 1...♔h8, 2 ♕h6 wins) 2 ♕g5+ *(1b)* saves a half-point.

1b) Black moves

The forced retreat 2...♔h8 is met by 3 ♕f6+ ♔g8 4 ♕g5+. White forces a draw by perpetual check.

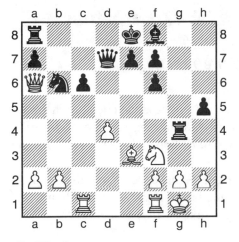

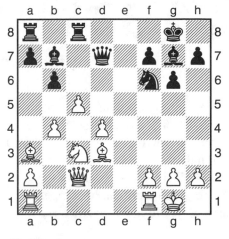

2) Black moves

Here the rook sacrifice gains a knight in return, but the outcome is the same: 1...♖xg2+ 2 ♔xg2 ♕g4+ 3 ♔h1 ♕xf3+ 4 ♔g1 ♕g4+ is a draw.

3) Black moves

A bishop sacrifice enables Black to force a welcome draw: 1...♗xg2 2 ♔xg2 ♕g4+ 3 ♔h1 ♕f3+ 4 ♔g1 ♕g4+.

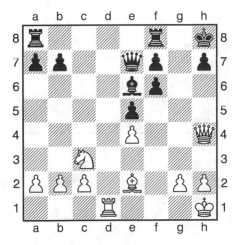

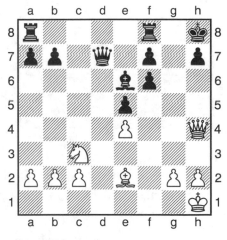

4a) White moves

The spectacular rook sacrifice 1 ♖d7! forces 1...♕xd7 (4b) (since if 1...♗xd7, 2 ♘d5 ♕d6 3 ♘xf6 threatens mate on h7).

4b) White moves

A draw by perpetual check follows: 2 ♕xf6+ ♔g8 3 ♕g5+ ♔h8 4 ♕f6+. A wonderful example of deflection as well as perpetual.

The ♘h6-f7 Perpetual

A white knight to the rescue...

This knight manoeuvre is a standard method of forcing perpetual check in the middle-game. It only requires the involvement of two white pieces, commonly queen and knight, although a partnership of rook and knight, or bishop and knight, is also seen occasionally.

Technically a game is not drawn on grounds of perpetual check, but rather by the rule of threefold repetition. In competitive play the rule is that if the same position with the same player to move occurs three times in a game, a draw may be claimed.

Typical Position for the ♘h6-f7 Perpetual

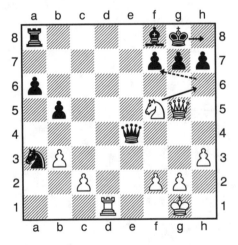

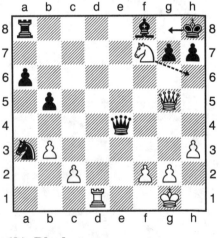

1a) White moves

White may be a piece down, but the manoeuvre 1 ♘h6+ ♚h8 2 ♘xf7+ *(1b)* sets the perpetual check in motion.

1b) Black moves

Black's king must return with 2...♚g8, when 3 ♘h6+ ♚h8 4 ♘f7+ repeats. A draw by threefold repetition is inevitable.

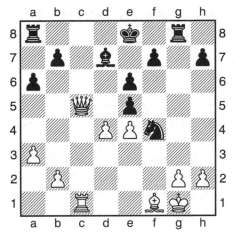

2) Black moves

In spite of earlier mislaying his queen, Black manages to sneak a draw by repetition: 1...♘h3+ 2 ♔h1 ♘f2+ 3 ♔g1 ♘h3+.

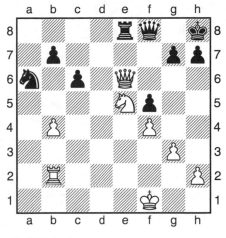

3) White moves

The white queen being under attack makes no difference, as 1 ♘f7+ ♔g8 2 ♘h6++ is a double check. A draw results after 2...♔h8 3 ♘f7+, etc.

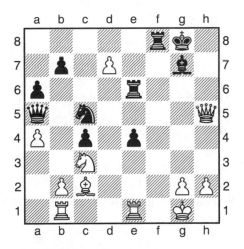

4a) Black moves

In the grandmaster game Timman-Wedberg, Malmö 2002, a draw was forced via the queen sacrifice 1...♘d3 2 ♕xa5 ♗d4+ 3 ♔h1 (4b).

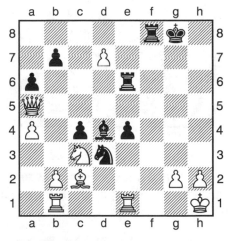

4b) Black moves

This bishop and knight double-act is worth noting. A perpetual check results: 3...♘f2+ 4 ♔g1 ♘h3++ 5 ♔h1 ♘f2+.

39   The ♗b5 & ♘c7+ Crusher (1)

A queen on c6 allows nasty tricks

The alarm bells should go off in almost any position where Black has a queen on the c6-square, and has not yet castled. There are compelling reasons why strong players generally do not develop the queen early on to such exposed squares.

If White has a knight on d5, there is one lethal tactic to watch out for. A white bishop moves to the b5-square – whether the bishop is protected or not – pinning Black's queen against his king. This is a crushing *decoy sacrifice*. If the bishop is captured, a knight check on c7 will fork the black king and queen.

Typical Position for the ♗b5 & ♘c7+ tactic

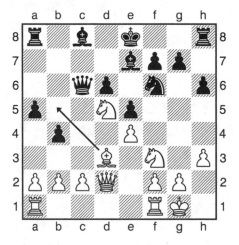

1a) White moves

All the ingredients are present for the tactical trick. 1 ♗b5 pins the black queen, and forces the capture 1...♛xb5 *(1b)*.

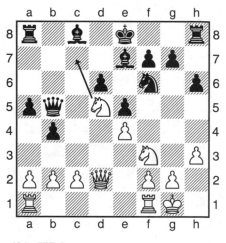

1b) White moves

There follows the knight fork 2 ♘c7+. The black king must move, and next White captures the queen with 3 ♘xb5.

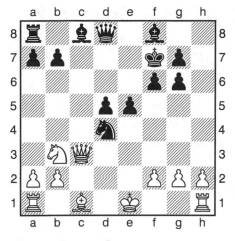

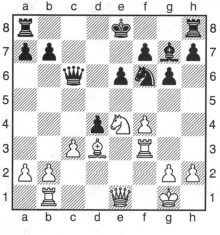

2) Black moves

The bishop decoy sacrifice 1...♗b4 forces 2 ♕xb4. After 2...♘c2+ Black wins by forking the white king and queen.

3) White moves

White's knight can start – and fork – from various squares, using the same basic principle: 1 ♗b5 ♕xb5 2 ♘d6+.

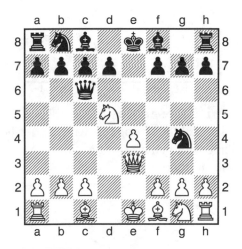

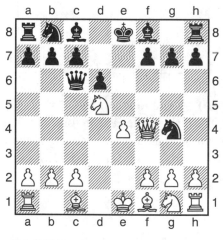

4a) White moves

After 1 ♕f4 (with a double attack on g4 and c7) it appears Black can defend against both threats with 1...d6 (4b).

4b) White moves

Not so! The crusher 2 ♗b5! wins instantly, as the queen is lost to a knight fork after 2...♕xb5 3 ♘xc7+.

The ♗b5 & ♘c7+ Crusher (2)

As old as the hills...

The ♘d5 and ♗b5 combination (as illustrated in the previous Tricky Tactic) can be effective even if White is not immediately pinning the black queen.

This was discovered over 165 years ago – our basic example comes from a match McDonnell-Labourdonnais, London 1834!

Typical Position for the ♗b5 & ♘c7+ tactic

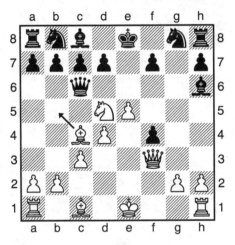

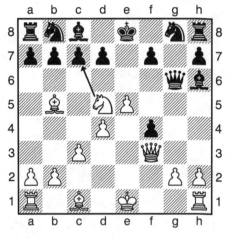

1a) White moves

The bishop offer 1 ♗b5 forces the black queen to abandon the defence of the c7-pawn with 1...♕g6 *(1b)* (if 1...♕xb5, 2 ♘xc7+).

1b) White moves

The knight swoops in with 2 ♘xc7+. White wins material, as the black king and rook are forked.

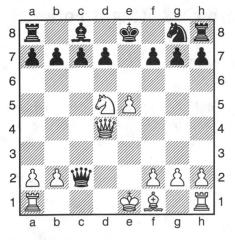

2a) White moves

An example of how to gain tempi in the opening. White plays 1 ♗d3 ♛c6 2 ♗b5! *(2b)* harassing the black queen.

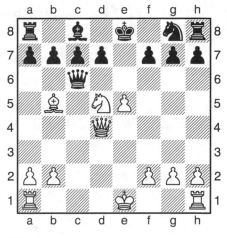

2b) Black moves

To keep defending the c7-pawn, Black plays 2...♛c2. But there follows 3 ♗a4! and White is winning.

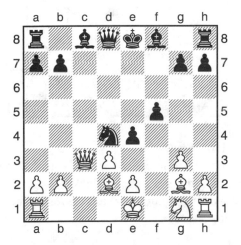

3a) Black moves

In the game (which went 1...♗b4 2 ♛c1! defending) Black missed a lovely interpolation: 1...e3! 2 ♗xe3 *(3b)*.

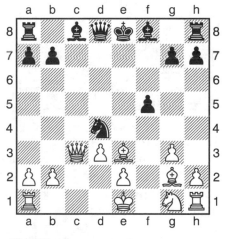

3b) Black moves

White has saved the bishop, but Black's pawn sacrifice has done its job. 2...♗b4 3 ♛xb4 ♘c2+ wins the white queen.

41 Queen Sacrifice & Knight Fork (1)

With the ♕xd5 and ♘c7+ trick

Where White has a knight on b5 in the opening, and Black has not yet castled, tactical opportunities often abound. The white knight is eyeing the c7-square for possible forks. A typical combination sees White winning material by first making a sacrifice on the d5-square.

This sacrifice frequently involves giving up the white queen. No matter, for a couple of moves later the queen is regained with interest.

Typical Position for the ♕xd5 and ♘c7+ trick

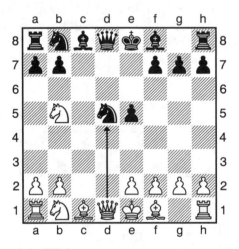 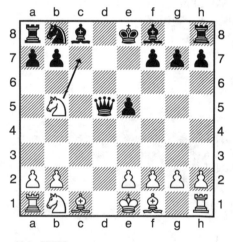

1a) White moves

In reply to the temporary queen sacrifice 1 ♕xd5, Black must recapture with 1...♕xd5 *(1b)* (or he has lost a knight for nothing).

1b) White moves

The knight check 2 ♘c7+ forks the black king and queen. Black's king must move, after which 3 ♘xd5 leaves White a piece ahead.

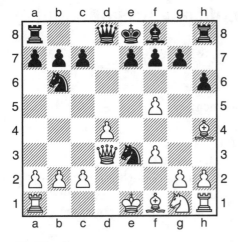

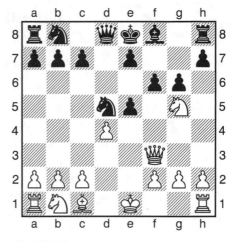

2) Black moves

A pawn down, Black appears to be under pressure. 1...♕xd4 saves the day, since 2 ♕xd4 is met with 2...♘xc2† followed by 3...♘xd4.

3) White moves

Black has fallen into an opening trap. 1 ♘e6 ♕d7 (1...♕d6 is the same) 2 ♕xd5! wins, since 2...♕xd5 is met by 3 ♘xc7+.

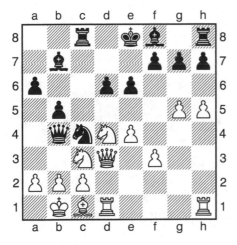

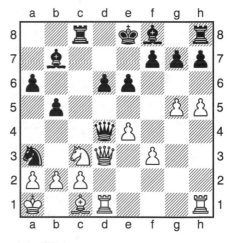

4a) Black moves

This pretty example (against a castled king) shows the motif in disguised form: 1...♘a3+ 2 ♔a1 ♕xd4! (4b).

4b) White moves

It is very nice how Black's preliminary knight check set up the forking formation. Black wins a pawn: 3 ♕xd4 ♘xc2+ 4 ♔b1 ♘xd4.

42 Queen Sacrifice & Knight Fork (2)

With the ♕h8+ and ♘f7+ trick

Watch out for this tactic after kingside castling when:
1) A white knight can move to the f7-square;
2) White's queen has access to the h8-square.

In such positions, if the black queen strays onto the wrong square (typically d8, d6 or e5) a striking queen sacrifice by White may be possible. The white queen can appear from any direction – down the h-file, along the eighth rank, or, less expectedly, down the long diagonal. Many beginners learn this tactic the hard way, losing a rook to it.

Typical Position for the ♕h8+ and ♘f7+ Trick

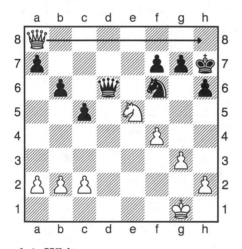

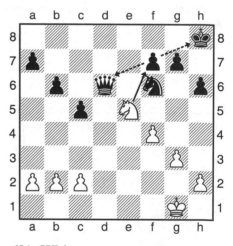

1a) White moves

The queen decoy sacrifice 1 ♕h8+ lures the black king to an unfortunate square. The capture 1...♔xh8 *(1b)* is forced.

1b) White moves

2 ♘xf7+ forks the black king and queen. Next move White regains the queen with 3 ♘xd6, remaining a pawn ahead.

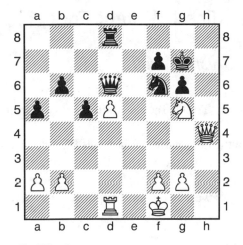

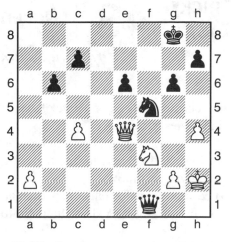

2) Black moves

Black's 1...♖h8? is a beginner's blunder. 2 ♕xh8+ ♔xh8 3 ♘xf7+ forks queen and king, and White has won a rook.

3) Black moves

The knight fork can occur on other squares. Here the motif enables a favourable queen swap: 1...♕h1+ 2 ♔xh1 ♘g3+ and next 3...♘xe4.

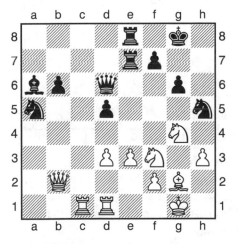

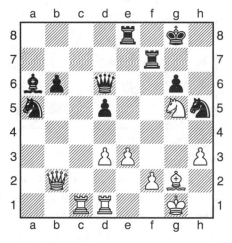

4a) White moves

This deep combination starts with some knight checks and a sacrifice: 1 ♘h6+ ♔h7 2 ♘xf7! ♖xf7 3 ♘g5+ ♔g8 (4b).

4b) White moves

After three preparatory moves, a familiar pattern emerges: 4 ♕h8+! ♔xh8 5 ♘xf7+ followed by 6 ♘xd6 gives White a winning position.

TRICKY TACTIC 43 — Queen Sacrifice & Knight Fork (3)

With the ♕h6+ and ♘f7+ trick

This sacrifice is a close relative of the previous two Tricky Tactics, though less common – and easier to miss.

Here the white queen is offered as a decoy on the h6-square. Sometimes Black can decline the sacrifice, only to find that acceptance is compulsory when the queen re-offers itself on h8 next move.

The version in diagram 2 is particularly evil. As well as losing two pawns, the victim ends up with two rooks humiliatingly forked.

Typical Position for the ♕h6+ and ♘f7+ Trick

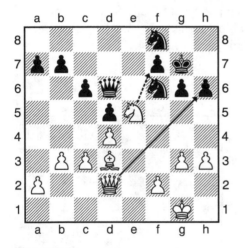

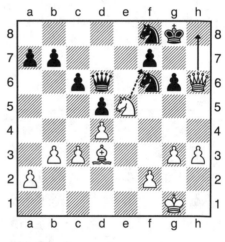

1a) White moves

The sacrifice 1 ♕xh6+ aims to decoy Black's king (since if 1...♔xh6, 2 ♘xf7+). So Black declines the queen with 1...♔g8 *(1b)*.

1b) Black moves

To no avail: White forces acceptance of the sacrifice by 2 ♕h8+! ♔xh8. With 3 ♘xf7+ followed by 4 ♘xd6, White wins two pawns.

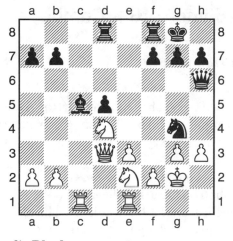

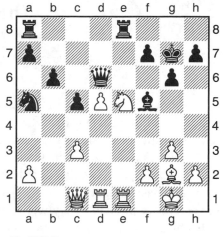

2) Black moves

Grandmaster Bent Larsen recently fell for this one: 1...♖xh3+ 2 ♔xh3 ♘xf2+ and next move 3...♘xd3 will embarrassingly fork the white rooks.

3) White moves

Here 1 ♕h6+ does not win out of hand, as 1...♔g8! avoids material loss. Black's h7-pawn prevents a follow-up queen check on h8.

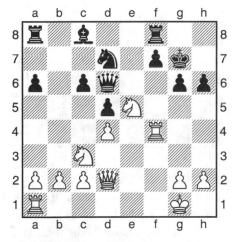

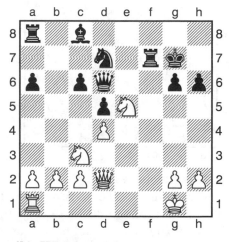

4a) White moves

The neat 1 ♖xf7+ ♖xf7 (4b) is both a clearance and a decoy sacrifice. White's queen now has a route to the h6-square.

4b) White moves

2 ♕xh6+ wins: on 2...♔g8 (2...♔xh6 3 ♘xf7+) 3 ♕h8+! ♔xh8 4 ♘xf7+ the white knight decisively forks the black king and queen.

The ♗h6 and ♘f6+ Combo

Common with either colour

This two-move-deep trap is a common motif in openings such as the English (for White) and the Closed Sicilian (for Black). There are various versions, depending on whether Black has castled, and whether he has a pawn on h6. The key elements are as follows:

1) Black has fianchettoed his king's bishop.
2) The black queen is on d7 and the black king is on g8 (or e8).
3) White has a knight on d5 (or e4) and a bishop on the c1-h6 diagonal.

In such positions White may well have the tactical shot ♗h6! available. The idea is that this bishop sacrifice cannot be accepted, due to a crushing knight fork on f6.

Typical Position of the ♗h6 & ♘f6+ Combination

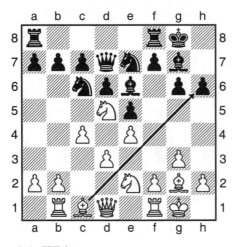

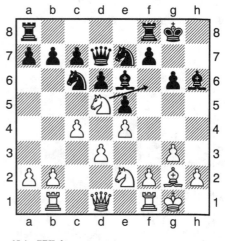

1a) White moves

The capture 1 ♗xh6 wins a pawn (if 1...♗xd5 or 1...♘xd5 then 2 ♗xg7). Instead 1...♗xh6? *(1b)* would be a disaster for Black.

1b) White moves

The black king and queen are forked by 2 ♘f6+. So Black cannot accept the bishop sacrifice, and loses the h-pawn for nothing.

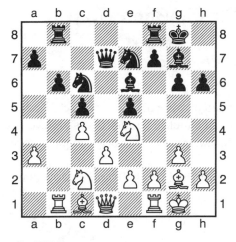

2) White moves

With the knight on e4, a 1 ♗xh6 combination is simpler to calculate. 1...♗xh6 is impossible due to the fork 2 ♘f6+.

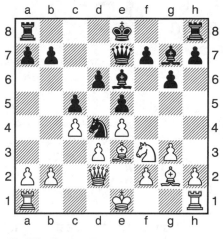

3) Black moves

A deadlier version arises if the victim is uncastled. 1...♗h3! typically wins rook for bishop after 2 0-0 ♘xf3+ 3 ♗xf3 ♗xf1.

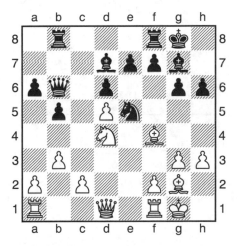

4a) Black moves

In this advanced version the white queen is lured to a forking square: 1...♗xh3! 2 ♗xh3 ♕xd4! (4b).

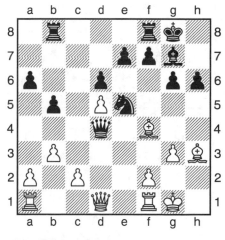

4b) White moves

Very imaginative. After 3 ♕xd4 comes 3...♘f3+ 4 ♔g2 ♘xd4, and Black emerges a pawn ahead.

An 'Elastic Band' Trap

Bouncing back to bag a pawn

There is a type of combination where an unexpected capture of a well-protected pawn is possible, because it exposes another enemy piece to attack. The 'elastic band' motif occurs when – after the defender exchanges the attacked piece – the original piece recaptures, springing back into safety.

   This trap is endemic in pawn-structures arising via the French Defence. Most players below club level would fall for this one.

Typical Position for an 'Elastic Band' trap

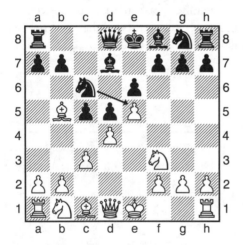

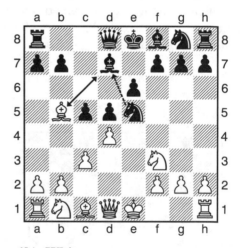

1a) Black moves

In this basic French Defence version the surprise capture 1...♞xe5! *(1b)* exploits the undefended white bishop on b5.

1b) White moves

A white pawn is lost. If 2 ♞xe5 (or 2 dxe5) comes 2...♝xb5, or 2 ♝xd7+ ♞xd7, and the black knight springs back to safety.

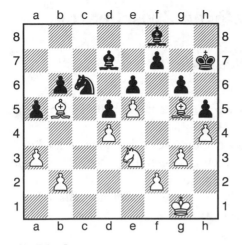

2) Black moves

Elastic bands still work in the end-game: 1...♘xe5 2 ♗xd7 (or 2 dxe5 ♗xb5) 2...♘xd7 and Black is a pawn up.

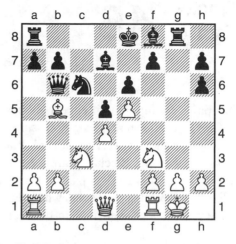

3) Black moves

The concept can rebound: here 1...♘xe5 2 ♘xe5 ♗xb5 3 ♕h5 ♖g7 4 ♖fe1 gives White a ferocious attack for the pawn.

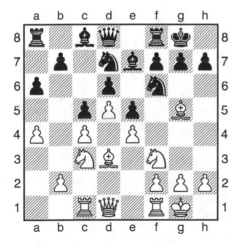

4a) Black moves

The bishop on g5 is defended. Nevertheless 1...♘xd5! (4b) was played, offering White three ways to capture the knight.

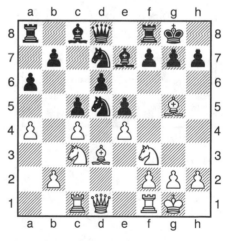

4b) White moves

There is no good answer to the cheeky pawn grab. For example, 2 ♗xe7 ♘xe7, or 2 ♘xd5 ♗xg5 3 ♘xg5 ♕xg5.

The ...♘xe4 Zwischenzug

Always look a leap ahead

This pawn-winning motif appears in positions where White has developed a bishop on g5 (or sometimes h4) exerting pressure on a black knight on f6.

Although the knight is not pinned (Black has a bishop on e7), the move ...♘xe4 is still a shock. How can Black capture the e-pawn, which is so clearly protected? It appears that White can swap bishops, and then win the knight on e4.

Black's nice idea is revealed when, delaying the recapture of the bishop, Black first interpolates the zwischenzug ('in-between-move') ...♘xc3.

Typical Position for the ...♘xe4 Zwischenzug

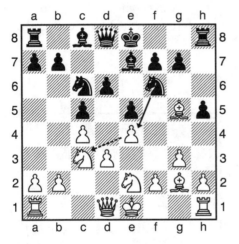 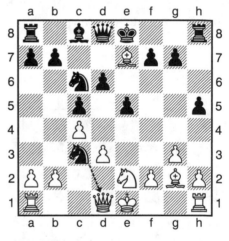

1a) Black moves

After 1...♘xe4 2 ♗xe7 (if 2 ♘xe4 then 2...♗xg5) Black reveals his *zwischenzug* with the move 2...♘xc3! *(1b)*.

1b) White moves

The white queen is attacked, and Black wins a pawn in all lines: 3 ♘xc3 ♗xe7, or 3 ♗xd8 ♘xd1 4 ♖xd1 ♔xd8.

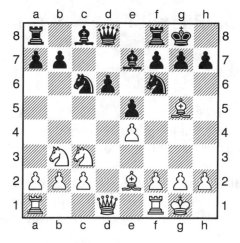

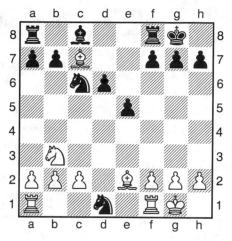

2a) Black moves

A common Sicilian Defence example: 1...♘xe4 2 ♗xe7? (trying for more than 2 ♘xe4 ♗xg5) 2...♘xc3 3 ♗xd8 ♘xd1 4 ♗c7 *(2b)*.

2b) Black moves

The black knight escapes with 4...♘xb2! 5 ♗xd6 ♖d8 6 ♗a3 ♘a4, and Black remains a pawn ahead.

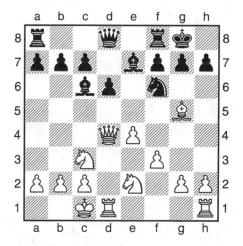

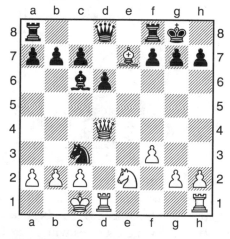

3a) Black moves

A white queen on d4 can also present a target. 1...♘xe4 2 ♗xe7 ♘xc3! *(3b)* still works, as Black threatens a killer fork on e2.

3b) White moves

Again White is losing a pawn, i.e. 3 ♘xc3 ♕xe7. Instead 3 ♗xd8? ♘xe2+ would fork the white king and queen.

Breaking the Pin with ...♘xe4 (1)

Unpinning and winning

In many positions White likes to place a bishop on g5, pinning the black knight on f6 against a black queen on d8. However, the very fact that the pin on the knight seems so strong can sometimes be White's undoing. Such pins can, on occasion, be dramatically broken, and this tactic shows how.

The basic example (below) is shown from Black's point of view. Of course there are many opening traps (such as Legall's Mate[1]) where White also uses the motif to win.

It is surprising how often these ...♘xe4 pin-breaks occur. But accurate calculation is essential, or a piece (or worse) could be lost for nothing.

Typical Position for Breaking the Pin with ...♘xe4

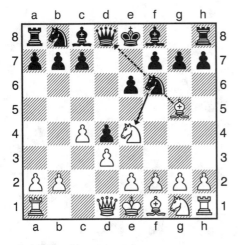
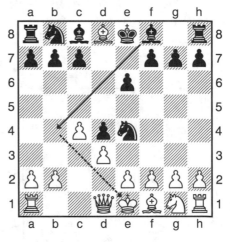

1a) Black moves

1...♘xe4 is a pin-break: Black ignores the attack on his queen. As 2 dxe4 fails to 2...♕xg5, White captures with 2 ♗xd8 *(1b)*.

1b) Black moves

The reply 2...♗b4+ is crushing. White must interpose with 3 ♕d2, and will end up more than a piece down after 3...♗xd2+.

---

1 Legall's famous Mate runs 1 e4 e5 2 ♘f3 d6 3 ♗c4 ♗g4 4 ♘c3 g6? 5 ♘xe5! ♗xd1 6 ♗xf7+ ♔e7 7 ♘d5 checkmate.

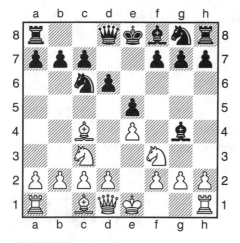

2) White moves

Sacrifices demand precise calculation. 1 ♘xe5? (thinking only of the line 1...♗xd1 2 ♗xf7+) proves to be a blunder after 1...♘xe5.

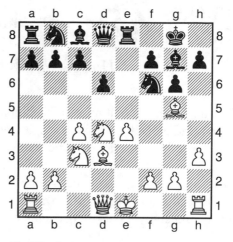

3) Black moves

Here the pin-break is helped by a discovered check on the e-file. 1...♘xe4 2 ♗xd8 (if 2 ♘xe4, then 2...♕xg5) 2...♘xc3+ and Black regains the queen.

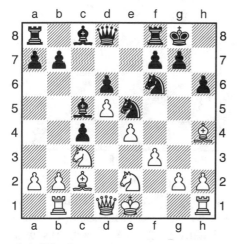

4a) Black moves

Black conjures up a stunning combination, aided by a second knight sacrifice: 1...♘xe4 2 ♗xd8 ♘xf3+!! *(4b)*.

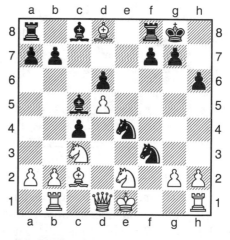

4b) White moves

Black Magic! If 3 gxf3, then 3...♗f2+ 4 ♔f1 ♗h3 is mate, or 3 ♔f1 ♘ed2+ 4 ♕xd2 (forced) 4...♘xd2+ and Black wins on material.

Breaking the Pin with ...♘xe4 (2)

Danger for White in the opening

This unpinning knight move is common in certain openings, such as the Sicilian and Nimzo-Indian Defences. So it is again presented from Black's point of view.

In the previous Tricky Tactic, the shock capture ...♘xe4 was possible because of checking or mating possibilities. Here we examine versions where Black *exploits the exposed position of a white queen sitting on d2 or c3.*

The tactic can be an unusual way to exchange queens – and it often wins material for Black, especially if the knight captured a pawn on e4. At all levels this is a classic point-winner.

Typical Position for Breaking the Pin with ...♘xe4

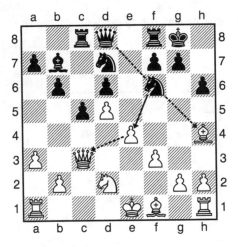

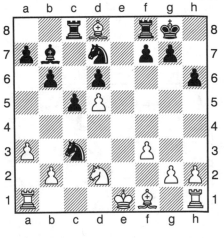

1a) Black moves

1...♘xe4! attacks the white queen on c3, enabling an unusual queen swap: 2 ♗xd8 (if 2 fxe4 or 2 ♘xe4, then 2...♛xh4+) 2...♘xc3 (*1b*).

1b) White moves

Although White can capture a minor piece with 3 bxc3, Black can respond in kind with 3...♖cxd8. Black has won a pawn.

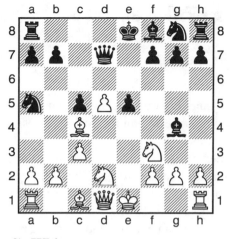

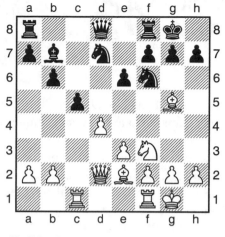

2) White moves

1 ♘xe5 captures a pawn and attacks the black queen on d7. 1...♗xd1 2 ♘xd7 leaves White a pawn ahead (if 2...♔xd7, 3 ♔xd1).

3) Black moves

The motif can be useful without winning material. Black eases a cramped game via 1...♘e4 2 ♗xd8 ♘xd2 3 ♘xd2 ♖fxd8.

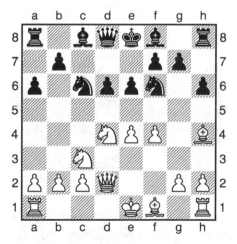

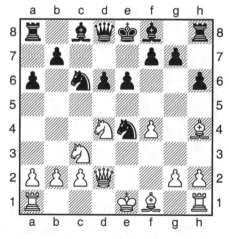

4a) Black moves

A Sicilian Defence trap. After 1...♘xe4 (4b) a key point is that the bishop on h4 is undefended (so if 2 ♘xe4 then 2...♕xh4+).

4b) White moves

Despite having many options, White will lose a pawn: 2 ♗xd8 ♘xd2 3 ♘xc6 bxc6 and now 4 ♔xd2 ♔xd8 or 4 ♗h4 ♘xf1.

109

The ♗c7 Queen Trap

Exploit a pin on the c-file

This trap has been a popular way for Black to lose quickly over many years. An example between famous players was the game Alekhine-Rubinstein, San Remo 1930 (position 1a).

The trick exploits a form of pin on the semi-open c-file. A white knight moves unexpectedly to the d5- or b5-square – often capturing a pawn in the process. This knight sacrifice is possible because, if the c-file is opened, the move ♗c7 will snare the black queen.

Black usually refuses to capture the knight, but the damage is done. White gains a winning position.

Typical Position for the ♗c7 Queen Trap

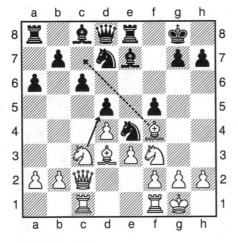

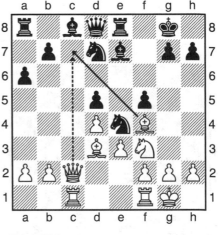

1a) White moves

The capture 1 ♘xd5! cleverly exploits a pin on the c-file. White wins a pawn for nothing, since 1...cxd5? (*1b*) would be disastrous for Black.

1b) White moves

2 ♗c7! traps the black queen, which is hemmed in by its own pieces and has no escape squares. White's bishop is defended now that the c-file is open.

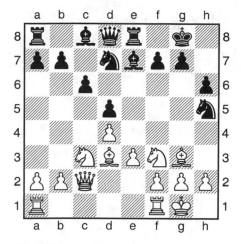

2) White moves

It makes no difference that the white bishop on g3 is attacked: 1 ♘xd5 ♘xg3 2 ♘xe7+! ♕xe7 3 hxg3 wins a pawn.

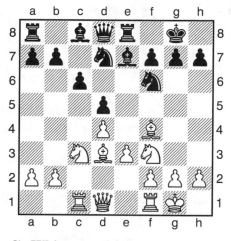

3) White moves

Here the trap is sprung via the b5-square. On 1 ♘b5! Black sheds material: 1...cxb5 2 ♗c7, or 1...♖f8 2 ♗c7 ♕e8 3 ♘d6 ♗xd6 4 ♗xd6.

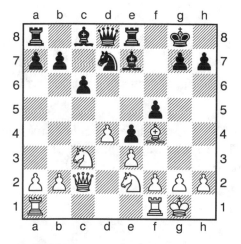

4) White moves

In this version Grandmaster Lajos Portisch found himself spoilt for choice: 1 ♘b5 and 1 ♘d5 are both strong moves!

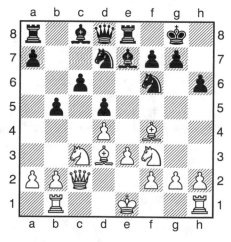

5) White moves

If White is uncastled, the trap may rebound. 1 ♘xb5? fails, as 1...cxb5 2 ♗c7 ♗b4+! frees the escape square e7 for the black queen.

Far-Advanced Pawns

Poised for greatness

A pawn reaching the seventh rank invariably opens up a wealth of exciting new tactical possibilities. Because the pawn is so close to the promotion square, the most extraordinary sacrifices can become possible. After all, what does it matter if a bishop, knight or even rook is given up, if promoting a pawn to a new queen becomes possible?

Typical Position for a Far-Advanced Pawn Combination

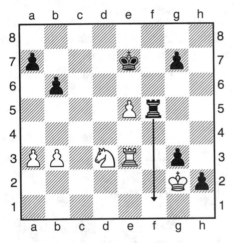

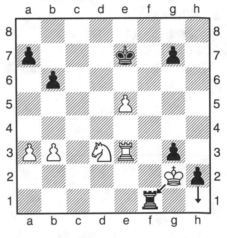

1a) Black moves

The rook offer 1...♖f1 *(1b)* shows a standard motif for assisting the black h-pawn to promote (if 2 ♔xf1, then 2...h1♕+ wins).

1b) White moves

The position is resignable for White. There is no way to prevent Black from making a new queen with 2...h1♕+.

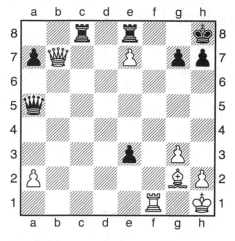

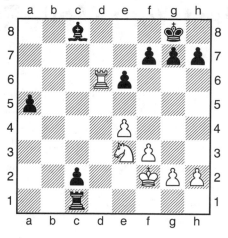

2) White moves

Far-advanced pawns are lethal in conjunction with back-rank mates. 1 ♕xc8 ♖xc8 2 ♖f8+ mates after 2...♖xf8 3 cxf8♕.

3) Black moves

The white threat (1 ♖d8 checkmate) is countered in an amazing way: 1...♖d1!! 2 ♘xd1 h6! and Black's c-pawn will promote.

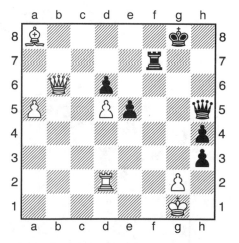

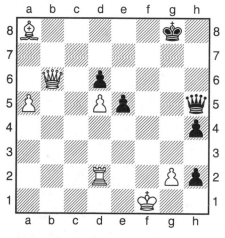

4a) Black moves

Another remarkable example: 1...♖f1+ 2 ♔xf1 h2! (4b) creates a position where the black pawn on h2 will queen by force.

4b) White moves

A rook and bishop ahead, White is lost: 3 ♕d8+ ♔g7 4 ♕e7+ ♕f7+ 5 ♕xf7+ ♔xf7 and the h2-pawn promotes next move.

Test Your Motif Recognition

The following eight combinations feature motifs covered in this book. Your task in this little test is to identify the principal motif involved. The key moves are given to you.

Select the one correct motif, from the choice of two given below each position. You'll need to think quite carefully about some of them. Even masters have been known to mix up the names of the themes they play so well!

Solutions on page 126.

Target Scores

Award yourself 1 point for each motif correctly identified.

All 8 Excellent motif recognition
6-7   Good motif recognition
4-5   Just above average
0-3   You'll need more luck in your games

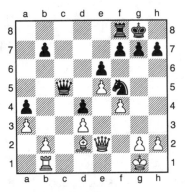

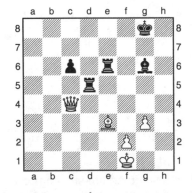

1) White plays 1 ♗b4.
Pin or *Skewer*?

2) Black plays 1...♗d3+.
Fork or *Skewer*?

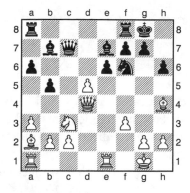

3) Black plays 1...♗c5.
Pin or *Fork*?

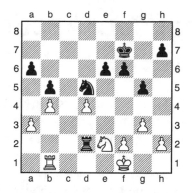

4) Black plays 1...♖xe2 2 ♔xe2 ♘c3+.
Desperado Sacrifice or *Knight Fork*?

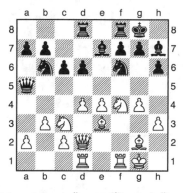

5) White plays 1 ♘cd5 ♕xd2 2 ♘xe7+.
Zwischenzug or *Kamikaze Queen*?

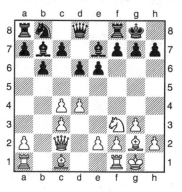

6) White plays 1 ♘g5 ♗xg5 2 ♗xb7.
Decoy Sacrifice or *Discovered Attack*?

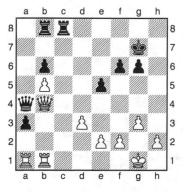

7) Black plays 1...♖c1+ 2 ♖xc1 ♕xb4.
Deflection or *Decoy*?

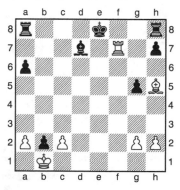

8) White plays 1 ♖xh7+.
Double Check or *Discovered Check*?

Test Your Tactics

The following 54 test positions are all taken from tournament games, and feature the motifs covered in this book. Your task is to find the combinative idea that either wins material, checkmates, or (in a small number of cases) saves a draw. Some of the positions are straightforward, and some of them are hard.

If you need a hint, then look up the *Tricky Tactic* listed next to each position, to see the main tactical idea that you should be looking for.

Solutions begin on page 126.

Target Scores

Award yourself 1 point for each combination correctly solved (without using the hints).

All 54	**Master standard**
49-53	**Tournament strength player**
40-48	**Excellent Tactic Ability**
31-39	**Good Tactical Ability**
23-30	**Promising – join a chess club!**
16-22	**Average**
8-15	**More practice needed**
0-7	**Try outdoor sports**

THE FORK

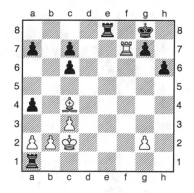

1) White wins

Hint: see Tricky Tactic 11

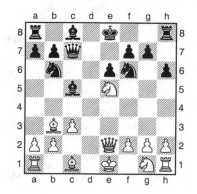

2) Black wins

Hint: see Tricky Tactic 15

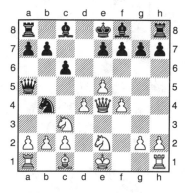

3) Black wins

Hint: see Tricky Tactics 2 & 21

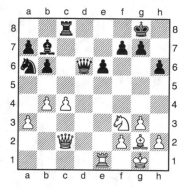

4) White wins

Hint: see Tricky Tactic 30

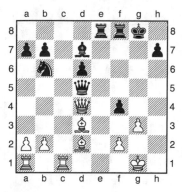

5) White wins

Hint: see Tricky Tactic 18

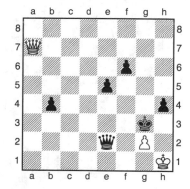

6) White draws

Hint: see Tricky Tactic 25

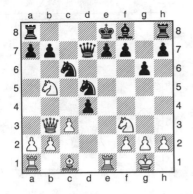

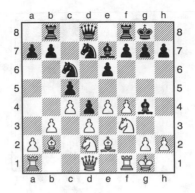

7) White wins

Hint: see Tricky Tactic 41

8) White wins

Hint: see Tricky Tactic 45

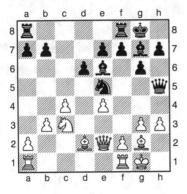

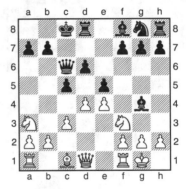

9) Black wins

Hint: see Tricky Tactic 44

10) White wins

Hint: see Tricky Tactic 48

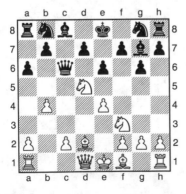

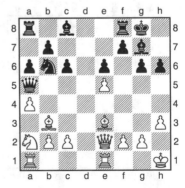

11) White wins

Hint: see Tricky Tactic 40

12) White wins

Hint: see Tricky Tactic 6

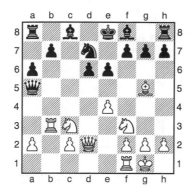

13) White wins
Hint: see Tricky Tactic 32

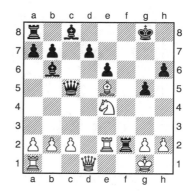

14) Black wins
Hint: see Tricky Tactic 12

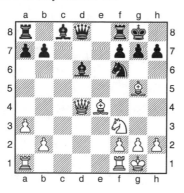

15) Black wins
Hint: see Tricky Tactic 31

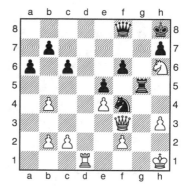

16) White wins
Hint: see Tricky Tactic 7

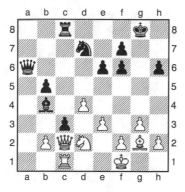

17) Black wins
Hint: see Tricky Tactic 50

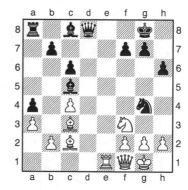

18) White wins
Hint: see Tricky Tactic 19

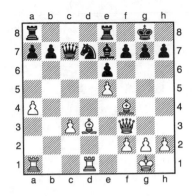

19) White wins
Hint: see Tricky Tactic 22

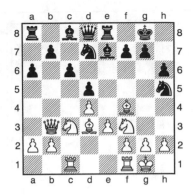

20) White wins
Hint: see Tricky Tactic 49

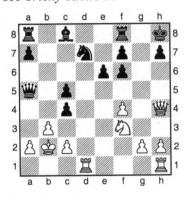

21) White draws
Hint: see Tricky Tactic 37

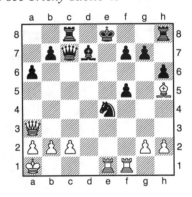

22) White wins
Hint: see Tricky Tactic 11

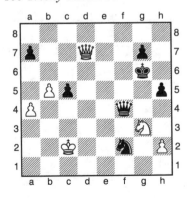

23) White wins
Hint: see Tricky Tactics 2 & 7

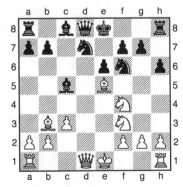

24) Black wins
Hint: see Tricky Tactic 14

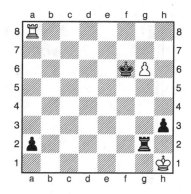

25) White draws
Hint: see Tricky Tactic 27

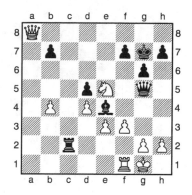

26) White wins
Hint: see Tricky Tactic 42

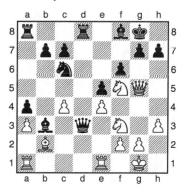

27) White draws
Hint: see Tricky Tactic 38

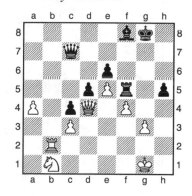

28) Black wins
Hint: see Tricky Tactic 17

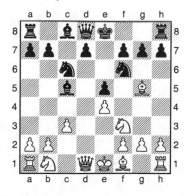

29) Black wins
Hint: see Tricky Tactic 16

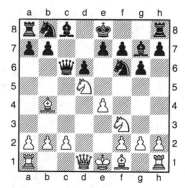

30) White wins
Hint: see Tricky Tactic 39

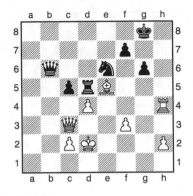

31) Black wins
Hint: see Tricky Tactic 3

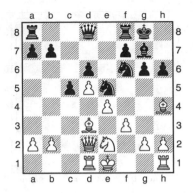

32) Black wins
Hint: see Tricky Tactic 48

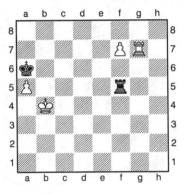

33) Black draws
Hint: see Tricky Tactic 26

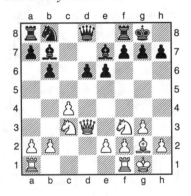

34) White wins
Hint: see Tricky Tactic 30

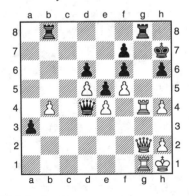

35) Black draws
Hint: see Tricky Tactic 50

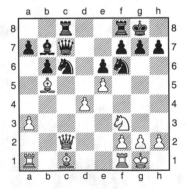

36) Black wins
Hint: see Tricky Tactic 34

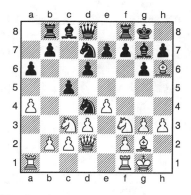

37) Black wins
Hint: see Tricky Tactic 44

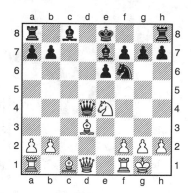

38) White wins
Hint: see Tricky Tactic 31

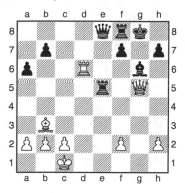

39) White draws
Hint: see Tricky Tactic 36

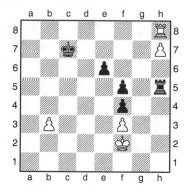

40) White wins
Hint: see Tricky Tactic 35

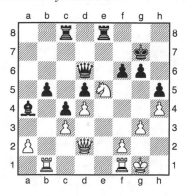

41) White wins
Hint: see Tricky Tactic 43

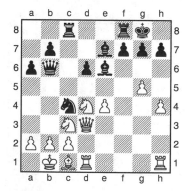

42) Black wins
Hint: see Tricky Tactic 41

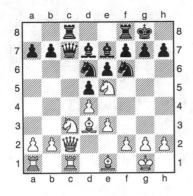

43) White wins
Hint: see Tricky Tactic 34

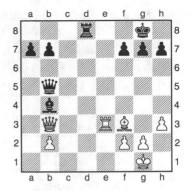

44) White wins
Hint: see Tricky Tactic 4

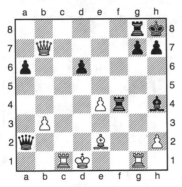

45) White wins
Hint: see Tricky Tactic 8

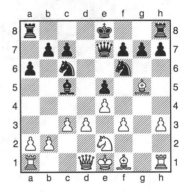

46) Black wins
Hint: see Tricky Tactic 47

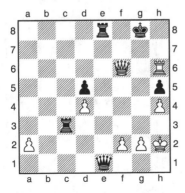

47) Black draws
Hint: see Tricky Tactic 29

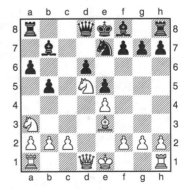

48) White wins
Hint: see Tricky Tactic 21

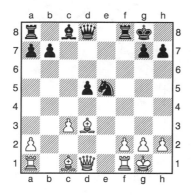

49) White wins
Hint: see Tricky Tactic 22

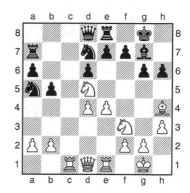

50) White wins
Hint: see Tricky Tactic 13

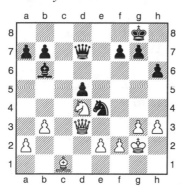

51) Black wins
Hint: see Tricky Tactic 43

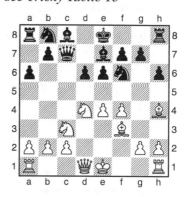

52) Black wins
Hint: see Tricky Tactic 46

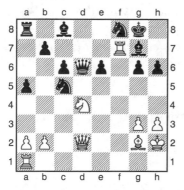

53) White wins
Hint: see Tricky Tactic 10

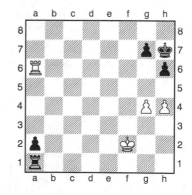

54) Black wins
Hint: see Tricky Tactic 35

Test Solutions

Motif Recognition Test

1. Skewer
2. Fork
3. Pin
4. Knight Fork

5. Zwischenzug
6. Discovered Attack
7. Deflection
8. Discovered Check

Test Positions

1. The *discovered check* 1 ♖f1+ wins Black's rook on a1 for nothing.

2. 1...♗xf2+ is a *decoy sacrifice* to win a pawn: 2 ♔xf2 (if 2 ♕xf2, then 2...♕xe5+) 2...♕xe5 3 ♕xe5 ♘g4+ followed by 4...♘xe5.

3. 1...f5 seeks to drive away the white queen from the defence of c2. After 2 exf6 ♗f5 3 ♕f3, 3...♘xc2+ is a winning *knight fork* of king and rook.

4. 1 ♘g5 unveils a *discovered attack* on the black bishop (since 1...hxg5 is met by 2 ♗xb7, forking rook and knight). White wins after 1...♗xg2 2 ♕h7+ ♔f8 3 ♕h8+ ♔e7 4 ♕xc8.

5. White *pins* the black queen with 1 ♗c4, as on 1...♘xc4, there comes 2 ♕xd5+.

6. White saves the draw by the trick 1 ♕e3+ ♕xe3 *stalemate*.

7. The temporary sacrifice 1 ♕xd5 wins a piece, as after 1...♕xd5 2 ♘c7+ White regains the queen with a knight fork.

8. 1 ♘xd4 wins a pawn using the *elastic band* motif. White threatens ♗xg4, and if 1...♗xe2 2 ♘xe2 the knight springs back to safety.

9. 1...♕xe2 2 ♘xe2 ♗xh3 is a pawn-winning *deflection sacrifice* based on a *knight fork*: if 3 ♗xh3, there comes 3...♘f3+ followed by 4...♘xd2.

10. White *breaks the pin* with 1 ♘xe5 ♗xd1 (1...dxe5 2 ♕xg4+) 2 ♘xc6 bxc6 3 ♖xd1, emerging a pawn ahead.

11. 1 b5 axb5 2 ♗xb5 runs the black queen out of squares: if 2...♕xb5, 3 ♘c7+ forks king and queen, while 2...♕c5 fails to 3 ♗b4.

12. 1 ♗d2 ♕c5 2 ♗b4 is a *skewer* of the black queen and rook.

13. 1 ♘d5 wins outright, as on 1...♕xd2 comes 2 ♘c7 checkmate.

14. Although Black's queen and rook are forked, the power of a *double check* decides: 1...♖f1++ 2 ♔xf1 ♕g1 mate.

15. Black wins a pawn with 1...♗xh2+ (a *discovered attack on the d-file*) 2 ♔xh2 ♕xd4 3 ♘xd4 ♘xe4.

16. The crushing *decoy sacrifice* 1 Rd8 wins the black queen after 1...Qxd8 2 Nf7+.

17. 1...cxd2 exploits Black's *far-advanced pawn*. White is lost after 2 Qxc8+ Nf8 (2...Bf8 and 2...Kg7 are just as good) 3 Qxa6 dxc1Q+.

18. 1 Qd3 (threatening Qh7+) 1...Qxd3 2 Re8+ is a neat *zwischenzug* to pin down the black pieces. After 2...Bf8 3 Bxd3 Black is losing material, i.e. 3...b6 4 Bf5.

19. A decoy sacrifice 1 Bxh7+ Kxh7 sets up the *queen fork* 2 Qd3+ winning a pawn, i.e. 2...Kg8 3 Qxd7 Qxc3 4 Qxb7.

20. 1 Nxd5 nabs a key central pawn, due to a *pin* on the c-file. If 1...cxd5, 2 Bc7 would trap the black queen.

21. Although a piece down, White draws by forcing *perpetual check on the f6- and g5-squares*: 1 Rxd7 Bxd7 2 Qxf6+ Kg8 3 Qg5+, etc.

22. 1 Rxe4+ fxe4 2 Rxf7 sets up a deadly *discovered check* in addition to mating threats. After 2...Qc5, 3 Rf5+ wins.

23. 1 Qxg7+ nets two pawns by means of a *decoy* sacrifice based on the *knight fork* 1...Kxg7 2 Nxh5+. Next move White continues 3 Nxf4 with a winning endgame.

24. 1...Bxf2+ wins a pawn, as 2 Kxf2 Ng4+ forks White's king and the bishop on e5.

25. After jettisoning his last pawn with 1 g7 Rxg7 (1...Rxg7 2 Rxa2 is a simple draw), White then saves the draw using the *rampant rook* motif: 2 Ra7+ Kf6 3 Ra6+ Ke5 4 Ra5+ Kd4 5 Ra4+ Kc3 6 Ra3+ Kb4 (6...Kb2 7 Rxa2+) 7 Ra4+! and the rook draws by continual checks. If Black ever captures the rook, the white king is stalemated.

26. A *decoy sacrifice* followed by a *knight fork* wins for White: 1 Qh8+ Kxh8 2 Nxf7+ and next move 3 Nxg5.

27. A pawn down, White bails out with the *perpetual check* 1 Nh6+ Kh8 2 Nf7+ Kg8 3 Nh6+, etc.

28. 1...Bc5 pins and wins the white queen.

29. 1...Bxf2+ 2 Kxf2 Nxe4+ wins a pawn by forking the white king and bishop.

30. White wins the black queen with a *pin* followed by a *knight fork*: 1 Bb5 Qxb5 2 Nc7+.

31. After 1...Rxe5 2 dxe5 Black picks up the loose white rook on h4 by means of the *queen fork* 2...Qd8+.

32. The pin-break 1...Nxe4 2 Bxd8 (if 2 Bxe4, then 2...Qxh4+) 2...Nxd2 is good for Black.

33. 1...Rxf7 saves the draw because Black would be stalemated after 2 Rxf7.

34. 1 Ng5 (threatening Qxh7 mate) 1...Bxg5 2 Bxb7 wins.

35. Black uses his *far-advanced pawn* to achieve a clever draw: 1...Qxg1+ 2 Qxg1 Rxg4 3 Qxg4 a2 4 Qg1 Rxb4 and now White must force perpetual check with 5 Qa7 Rb1+ 6 Kg2 a1Q 7 Qxf7+.

36. 1...Nxe5 wins a key pawn, as White must deal with a *discovered attack* on his queen down the c-file. After 2 Qxc7 Black plays 2...Nxf3+ (a *zwischenzug*) 3 gxf3 Rxc7.

127

37. After 1...♘xf3+ 2 ♗xf3 ♘e5 the retreat 3 ♗g2 appears to defend the h3-pawn, but the pawn grab 3...♗xh3 is nevertheless possible (4 ♗xh3 ♘f3+ would fork king and queen).

38. 1 ♗b5+ wins the black queen with a *discovered attack on the d-file* from White's queen on d1.

39. 1 ♖xg6+ forces a draw by *perpetual check*: 1...hxg6 2 ♕xg6+ ♔h8 3 ♕h6+ ♔g8 4 ♕g6+, etc.

40. The *rook endgame skewer* 1 ♖a8 wins instantly, since 1...♖xh7 is met by 2 ♖a7+.

41. The *queen decoy sacrifice* 1 ♕h6+ is crushingly strong, as after 1...♔xh6 2 ♘f7+ White will regain the queen with 3 ♘xd6 – and fork the black rooks.

42. Black wins a pawn using a *queen sacrifice followed by a knight fork*: 1...♘a3+ 2 ♔a1 ♕xd4 3 ♕xd4 ♘xc2+ 4 ♔b1 ♘xd4.

43. 1 ♘xd5 wins a pawn: 1...♘xd5 (1...♕xc2? 2 ♘xe7+) 2 ♕xc7 ♖xc7 3 ♖xc7 ♘xc7 4 ♘xd7.

44. 1 ♖e7 exploits a pin of the black bishop (1...♗xe7 2 ♕xb5). White wins due to the double threat of 2 ♕xf7+ and 2 ♖xb7.

45. 1 ♕xg7+ is a pretty queen sacrifice that *deflects* the black rook off the back rank. Mate follows after 1...♖xg7 2 ♖c8+.

46. 1...♘xe4 *breaks the pin*. If 2 ♗xe7 then 2...♗f2 is checkmate, or otherwise Black wins a pawn, i.e. 2 fxe4 ♕xg5 with a mighty attack to boot.

47. Black's king is potentially stalemated, allowing a remarkable draw involving a *kamikaze queen* and two *rampant rooks*: 1...♕h1+ (1...♕g1+ leads to the same) 2 ♔xh1 ♖e1+ 3 ♔h2 ♖h1+ 4 ♔xh1 ♖h3+ 5 ♔g1 ♖h1+ forcing 6 ♔xh1 stalemate.

48. 1 ♗b6 wins. After the attacked black queen moves, White has 2 ♘c7+, a *knight fork*.

49. 1 ♗xh7+ ♔xh7 2 ♕h5+ is a *queen fork*. White is a pawn ahead after 2...♔g8 3 ♕xe5.

50. 1 ♗xe7 wins, as on 1...♖xe7 2 ♖c8 ♕xc8, 3 ♘xe7+ wins the black queen with a knight fork.

51. 1...♕xh3+ wins two pawns by utilizing a *knight fork*: 2 ♔xh3 (2 ♔g1 ♕h1+ forces the same line) 2...♘xf2+ 3 ♔g2 ♘xd3 4 exd3 ♗xd4.

52. 1...♘xe4 2 ♗xe7 ♘xc3 is a *zwischenzug* which wins Black a pawn.

53. 1 ♖xg7+ ♔xg7 2 ♘f5+ uses a *discovered attack* from the white queen to win the black queen (if 2...gxf5 or 2...exf5 then 3 ♕xd6).

54. 1...♖h1 wins by means of a *rook endgame skewer* after 2 ♖xa2 ♖h2+.